LIVING
LIKE
JESUS

Become
Everything
He Intended
You to Be

Foreword

by

Bill Bright

LIVING LIKE JESUS

Become Everything He Intended You to Be

Compiled and Edited by
James O. Davis and Ken Horn

Cutting Edge International
Orlando, Florida

James O. Davis
P. O. Box 411605
Melbourne, FL 32941-1605
www.JamesODavis.org

In Dedication

To Ray and Barbara Horwege whose lives have taught me so much about living like Jesus in the ministry.

~Ken Horn

To Christian martyrs who teach me the value of persistent character; to my late son, James Paul William Davis, who taught me the value of passionate commitment for he was born on Valentine's Day; and to Jesus Christ who taught me the value of a priceless commission.

~James O. Davis

CONTENTS

FOREWORD

For more than 55 years, it has been my privilege to follow in the footsteps of my Lord and Savior, Jesus Christ. It has been a joyful adventure overflowing with blessings without measure. Contrary to what many, even believers, often think, Christianity is not a penalty that one has to endure in order to qualify for heaven but rather an incredible adventure which has no equal. I did not just surrender my life to Christ so I could go to heaven but also that I might personally know and experience an intimacy with the Creator of more than 100 billion galaxies. Not only did He create our universe, but He also came to live and die for me upon a tiny, insignificant speck of sand called earth. The fact that He wishes to have fellowship with you and me is truly an indescribable joy.

One of the greatest truths He has taught me is this: Christianity is not what I do for Christ but what I allow Him to do through me. This was made clear to me more than 50 years ago when my wife Vonette and I signed a contract together to become slaves of Jesus Christ. We committed our lives to follow Him no matter what He called us to do or where He called us to go, surrendering up all of our personal rights and passions, allowing Him to do whatever He desired with our lives. At that time, we could not imagine the incredible adventure that lay before us.

In the spring of 1951, as a businessman and student at Fuller Theological Seminary, the Lord gave me a vision for Campus Crusade for Christ. I knew, clearly and unequivocally, that my awesome, powerful God was calling me to help fulfill the Great Commission during my lifetime. Today, through the ministries of Campus Crusade for Christ, there are over 25,000 full-time staff, more than 550,000 trained volunteer staff, reaching 191 countries worldwide for our great God and Savior. To Him be all praise and glory!

There have been countless blessings during that time as well as many challenges. One that I am experiencing at the time of this writing is a diagnosis of pulmonary fibrosis, an ailment afflicting the lungs for which medicine has no cure. But my hope and confidence is in the Lord! I know that He is able to heal me if He chooses to do so and that He will provide the strength necessary to finish the tasks to which He has called me. As a follower of our Lord Jesus Christ, I cannot lose. When I die, I will go to be with the Lord. Glorious! While I live, I will continue to glorify Him. He is so faithful!

There will come a day in the future when you will hear that Dr. Bill Bright has died. However, whenever the Lord has ordained this to happen, I encourage you to rejoice in the fact that I have finished the race that the Lord had marked out for me. We have only one life to live, and I want to live it to the fullest for His glory and honor. Vonette and I are determined to press on and not give up!

Living Like Jesus will inspire you to follow closely after our leader, Jesus Christ. He is the only one who deserves our unyielding, unswerving devotion every day for the rest of our lives. You will be encouraged in your personal pilgrimage in three areas—character, commitment, and commission. The book also addresses the vast differences between "being a character" and "having character," between "wearing a cross" and "bearing a cross," and between the "great omission" and "Great Commission."

My sincere desire is that you experience the same marvelous joy that I have found in surrendering my life to serve as a slave of our Lord Jesus Christ. An adventure waits you as you follow in His footsteps and fulfill His plan for your life. Truly, there is no higher, more worthy calling in all of history.

Bill Bright
Founder and President
Campus Crusade for Christ

ACKNOWLEDGMENTS

Special thanks to Peggy Horn, Sheri Davis, Debra Petrosky, Matt Key, Ann Floyd, Shirley Speer, and Richard Schoonover.

INTRODUCTION

When Jesus, the Son of God, came to earth clothed in human flesh, the heavenly hosts rejoiced; and peace and joy touched the realm of fallen man. But amidst the celebration, a Shadow was cast across the manger where the infant Jesus lay—a long Shadow, as though cast by the rising sun. This Shadow that first touched the corner of the Bethlehem cattle stall would remain over Jesus all His life.

In His childhood, the Shadow was there.

In His youth, the Shadow was there.

In His early manhood, the Shadow was there.

The tools of the carpenter passed through the Shadow.

When baptized by John, He was baptized in the Shadow.

When the Spirit descended as a dove and anointed Him for ministry—for His earthly mission—the dove rested on Him in the Shadow. When Jesus healed, He healed in the Shadow. Every man, woman, or child He touched was touched in the Shadow. Every step Jesus took, He took in the Shadow—an ever-decreasing Shadow as the day dawned and Jesus drew ever nearer to the Shadow's source.

Sometimes the Shadow was darker than at other times. Indeed, the Messiah was "a Man of sorrows and acquainted with grief."[1] The Shadow penetrated the dark of night; though short, it was at its darkest when Jesus prayed in the Garden of Gethsemane, "Let this cup pass from Me; nevertheless, not as I will, but as You will."[2]

Now Jesus is betrayed, arrested, forsaken—and from this point onward, every step He took would be directly toward the source of the Shadow. Into the presence of Annas, former high priest, they led Jesus—and the Shadow shortened.[3]

Now He stands before the high priest Caiaphas and the Jewish leaders, those "whitewashed tombs" that would pass judgment on the Son of God. And with the rending of the high priest's garments and the verdict "worthy of death," the Shadow shortened. Those who held Him mocked, spit upon, and beat the Lamb of God. They asked Him to name His tormenters; and though blindfolded, He knew—His attackers stood in the Shadow.[4]

Those nearest Him had run from the Shadow when the Lord was taken. His disciples had known there was a Shadow over Jesus' life; but they hadn't understood what cast it though He tried to help them understand.

Peter could not make up his mind; he weaved in and out of the Shadow, ran from it, then followed afar off— and denied his Friend three times.[5] (After Pentecost, that Shadow would be Peter's life—and, ultimately, his death.)

When our Lord's final day dawned and He stood silent before the Sanhedrin for the formal, predetermined death sentence, the Shadow was ever so short.[6]

Judas, His betrayer, hanged himself, to his eternal loss, where the Shadow could never touch him.[7]

Now four short steps would bring the King of kings to the source of the Shadow He had walked in all His life.

First, before Pilate. It seemed as if the Shadow weakened when Pilate said, "I find no fault in this Man."[8]

Next, before Herod, Jesus is silent. He would do nothing

to banish the Shadow though it was in His power. He is mocked and robed in finery.[9]

Back in Pilate's judgment hall, the Shadow could barely be seen, it was so short. Something in Pilate caused him to ask, "Shall release the King of the Jews?"

"Release Barabbas," the murderer, they cried—and "crucify Jesus."[10]

Now the soldiers led Him away, scourged Him, and clothed Him in purple. As the crown of thorns was pressed down across the Savior's brow, the Shadow began to be colored red. They struck His head and spit upon Him. They knelt and "worshipped" Him: "Hail, King of the Jews," they mocked.[11]

Now it was time for Jesus to meet His destiny—and ours. The Shadow that had been cast across eternity prepared to envelop "the Lamb slain from the foundation of the world." The final step that remained to meet the source—where He would drink the cup—was taken at the rough insistence of the soldiers, though He would have gone freely.[12] Jesus' final step before the Shadow covered Him fell on the Via Dolorosa, the "Way of Suffering."[13]

The Shadow now was as small as it had ever been. And yet it was intense, massive, looming. Jesus now stands directly beneath it. It touches no one else. Above Him, its source descends; the Shadow intensifies until the Shadow meets its source when on the strong shoulders of our gentle Lord the weight is placed—of the Cross. "They took Jesus... and He, bearing His cross, went out."[14] The Shadow that had traced its path through all of His 33 years on earth rested upon Jesus, "the Light of the world," and on Him alone. Jesus stood alone in the spotlight of the Shadow of the cross.

All His life, Jesus had been moving resolutely toward the cross. And now He bore its full weight.

How blessed in all of history is Simon of Cyrene who, when our Lord fell, stood under the Shadow and bore the weight of the cross. Jesus' physical strength could not match His spiritual strength for He had "humbled Himself and became obedient to...the death of the cross."[15] And the Via Dolorosa became the "Way of the Cross."

At Golgotha, at 9 a.m., nails are driven into the hands and feet of the Creator of the universe; the Lord and King on the cross is lifted. As it drops, it is not just His own weight that tears at His flesh—but the weight of sin of each and every person to walk the earth in all ages.

As the Sinless One—the only perfect man—hung between heaven and hell, He gazed at His tormenters with eyes of love—and saw you and me. Who put Jesus on the cross? The Jews did. The Romans did. I did. And you did.

The first words of Jesus from the cross were not: "Father, send 12 legions of angels" or "Smite my enemies" or even "Let this cup pass." They were, "Father, forgive them, for they do not know what they do."[16] No, I could not bear that weight had He not prayed that. At that moment, the cross cast its Shadow across His crucifiers, across soldiers, across the thieves on either side. It fell on onlookers, even on unfaithful disciples. It encircled the globe. The Shadow was cast back through time, clear to the day of Adam and Eve's fall; and it was cast forward to touch the Day of Pentecost. The Shadow raced across time. Today the Shadow is everywhere.

As the sun rose over Calvary, the Shadow of the cross was in motion. Christ died at noon, sun overhead, His life and death now fixed eternally to the cross. The instrument that brought death to the Son of God brought life to the sons of men. With the setting sun, the Way of the Cross stretched to eternity future. On the day of crucifixion, the Shadow was of Jesus on the cross. With the rising Son, the pattern of the Shadow is of the cross alone. If Jesus had not risen from the dead, there would be only darkness in that Shadow. And so now the cross gives life.

"Beneath the cross of Jesus I fain would take my stand; The shadow of a mighty Rock within a weary land, A home within the wilderness, A rest upon the way, From the burning of the noonday heat and the burden of the day."[17]

Living like Jesus means standing in the Shadow of the cross. It means walking in the Way of the Cross. And it means taking up your own cross.[18] Faithful disciples must follow Christ this way. Are you willing? Jesus took His cross for you. It weighed much more than yours. There will be no Simon of Cyrene to help you lift your cross should you stumble; but there will be the strong arms of Jesus with you, in the Shadow.

The chapters of this book contain the combined efforts of 32 modern-day disciples of Jesus to assist the reader along his or her own journey in following Christ—in living like Jesus, in the Shadow of His cross.

~Ken Horn

INTRODUCTION

How does one go about living like Jesus on a daily basis? Among the many grand and glorious principles taught by Jesus Christ, the second-mile principle completely showcases the dynamics of true discipleship. In the middle of the Sermon on the Mount, Jesus said, "If someone forces you to go one mile, go with him two mile" (Matthew 5:41, NIV). It is the second-mile principle that will put a smile on our faces, a spring in our steps, and a song in our hearts. The first mile is the trial mile; the second mile is the smile mile. The key to living life with a smile is a Christ-centered life. It has been said, "A person wrapped up in himself makes a very small package."

As you begin to read *Living Like Jesus*, I wish to provide several cognitive reasons for going the second mile in your discipleship. First, the second mile is the *character mile*. What was Jesus talking about when He said, "If someone forces you to go one mile, go with him two miles"? In Jesus' day, the Romans had a practice they had learned from the Persians about 600 years earlier. This practice was to subjugate a people who had been conquered through war.

If a Roman soldier saw a Jewish man or boy, he could command him to carry his backpack or burden. The Jewish male was required by law to comply for a mile. However, most Jews would not bear this burden one inch farther than the law required. This law caused terrible resentment among the Jews toward the Roman government.

Can you imagine how the Jews felt when Jesus said, "Go with him two miles"? No doubt, the audience said, "He must be jesting. Does He really expect us to do more than the law requires?" In essence, Jesus was saying that His disciples needed to do more than the legalists who do no more than what is required of them.

The principle of the second mile is to do more than is required or expected. Jesus is saying that any pagan or unsaved person can go one mile (vv. 46-47). The first mile is to love those who love us. The second mile is to love those who do not love us. We must always remember that life is lived on three levels. The *hellish level* is to return evil for good. The *human level* is to return good for good and evil for evil. The *heavenly level* is to return good for evil. The second mile is to return good for evil.

When a Jew is carrying the soldier's backpack for the first mile, he is a slave. However, when he chooses to carry the burden for a second mile, he then takes control of the situation. The character mile moves him from slave to master. The first mile is the have-to mile, but the second mile is the want-to mile.

The second mile is also the *commitment mile*. We go the first mile out of legalism but continue the second mile out of love. To live like Jesus, we must go the second mile when we experience *personal degradation* (vv. 38-39). The first mile is to give place to revenge, but the second mile is to give place to love. Jesus said, "If someone strikes you on the right cheek, turn to him the other also." Has someone treated you disrespectfully before others? If so, this is an appropriate opportunity to go the second mile. The best way to get rid of an enemy is to make a friend out of him.

Furthermore, the commitment mile includes *personal defeat* (v. 40). Jesus is talking about a legal settlement. In this legal matter, a brother has been found guilty. He has been required to give his shirt. In essence, Jesus is saying, "If you know you have done wrong, do not simply try to rectify the wrong by fulfilling the law but go the second mile. If you are wrong, then apologize, get right with your brother and God, and go the second mile."

Not only does the second mile include personal degradation and personal defeat but also *personal dedication* (v. 42). We are to have a giving spirit. We are not simply to pay our bills but also give to those who are in real need. To live like Jesus, we go the second mile when others have wronged us, when we have wronged others, and when there are serious financial needs.

Third, the second mile is the *commission mile*. I have been working with people long enough to observe that all successful people long enough to observe that all successful people live by the second-mile principle. The first mile is crowded, but the second mile is not busy at all.

Imagine two different scenes. In the first scene, a Roman soldier commands a Jewish man to carry his backpack for a mile. The first Jewish male becomes extremely upset as he picks up the soldier's burden and begins to carry it. As he carries the backpack, he talks in angry tones to the soldier. At the end of the mile, he throws the burden down and returns home, full of rage, hatred, and anger.

The second scene is the complete opposite. As soon as the Roman solider commands the Jewish male to carry his burden, he responds with a warm Christian greeting. In his heart, he truly wants to win this soldier to Jesus Christ. Along the way, he encourages conversation with the soldier. At the end of the first mile, the Jewish person says, "If you do not mind, I would be honored to carry your burden for a second mile."

Can you imagine the incredulous look on the soldier's face when hears these words? The Roman soldier says, "There is something different about you. Most Jewish men become angry when I command them to carry my backpack. What makes you different from the others?"

The man responds, "On one occasion, I heard Jesus Christ teach on the second-mile principle. So I am doing what Jesus Christ commanded me to do."

The soldier responds, "Who is Jesus Christ?"

The Jewish man answers, "He is the Messiah and Savior of the world."

By the time they reach the end of the second mile, this Jewish man has shared the gospel with this Roman soldier. The second mile is the witnessing mile.

I am convinced that more souls would be saved if we lived by the second-mile principle. Jesus went the second mile for us. Why would we want to live on the trial mile when we can live on the smile mile?

As you read *Living Like Jesus*, may you be encouraged to live on the second mile—the one that brings a smile.

~James O. Davis

1

To Change the World

D. JAMES KENNEDY

"And when they found them not, they drew Jason and certain brethren unto the rulers of the city, crying, These that have turned the world upside down are come hither also" (Acts 17:6, KJV).

The president of one of our great theological seminaries, at a meeting with the chairman of an accreditation committee, was asked what the purpose of the institution was.

The president replied: "The purpose of this institution is to change the world."

The committee member exclaimed, "No, no. I mean, what is the purpose of your school here?"

The president reiterated: "The purpose of our school is to change the world."

Now this secular chairman didn't particularly care for that idea, but repeated questioning failed to shake the gentleman from his position; he was there for the singular purpose of changing the world.

I don't know what your purpose in life is, but I share the same purpose as the president of that institution. My purpose, and I hope yours, is nothing less than to change the world. I expect this world will be different when I leave it than when I came into it because of the power of the gospel of Jesus Christ and the might of the Holy Spirit.

When Paul and Silas came to Thessalonica, a group of lewd men, of the baser sort, cried out in great dismay, "These that have turned the world upside down are come hither also" (Acts 17:6).

Would that the world today looked upon Christians as those who were turning the world upside down.

Is the great passion and desire of your heart to turn the world upside down for Jesus Christ? Or, should I say, is your purpose to turn it right side up? It's already upside down!

"Well," you say, "that's far beyond my ability. What could I do? Actually, I'm just a layman. I might teach a Sunday school class or something, but I couldn't really think about changing the world."

SPIRITUAL MULTIPLICATION

Perhaps such a thought went through the mind of Edward Kimball. He taught a Sunday school class composed of a small group of teenage boys—not exactly the kind of activity that was likely to change the world. One day he decided he would speak personally to one of the young lads about Christ. It didn't seem to him that the boy really knew the Savior. He went to the shoe store where the lad had a part-time job. But Kimball was shy, and a little voice inside of him was saying, *Why don't you find a more convenient time? Perhaps you could talk to him in church next Sunday.* But something inside also said, *No, do it now!* He mustered up his courage, walked through the front door of the store, and asked to speak to this young man who was in the stockroom putting shoes on the shelf. Kimball went back, engaged him in conversation, and finally led him to Christ right there among the shoes. This young man was going to change many a soul before he was finished with life. His name: Dwight L. Moody. He became one of the greatest preachers and evangelists ever. His ministry changed the face of the world, gave rise to the Moody Bible Institute, the Moody radio station, and the *Moody* publication, among other things. Thousands of missionaries have gone all over the world because of his ministry.

When Moody was in England, he influenced a young man by the name of F. B. Meyer who also became a great preacher of the gospel. Meyer came to America and preached in Moody's school in Massachusetts. There he had a tremendous impact on a man named J. Wilbur Chapman who, in turn, became a great evangelist. When he gave up his evangelistic work to go into the pastorate, he turned it over to a young man whom he had influenced by the name of Billy Sunday who became another Dwight Moody and changed the face of this nation. He went to Charlotte in 1924 and conducted a great evangelistic meeting. A number of men who were converted formed an organization and in 1932 held another evangelistic meeting to which they invited as speaker, Mordecai Ham. As Ham preached in Charlotte, a 16-year-old boy heard the gospel and, during the singing of the last stanza of a hymn, yielded his heart to Christ. His name: Billy Graham.

Who could begin to number the tens of millions of people who have been influenced by all of those great ministers down through the years who were influenced by...Edward Kimball? Who is he? Well, in heaven he will be a star. What could have happened in this world if he had approached the shoe store that day and said, "No, I'll do it another time," and gone home? Who can calculate the impact upon this world that his disobedience to the Great Commission would have created?

ARE YOU CONCERNED?

These are they who have turned the world upside down: people who cared enough to speak for Christ. Do you have that concern?

Those of us who lived through it will never forget an incident that took place April 1964 in New York City. A young woman coming home at night approached the front door of her apartment building and was accosted by a man. He slashed her with a knife. She screamed at the top of her voice. Then he cut her again. She screamed, "O my God, somebody help me! Please help me! I'm dying! I'm dying! Somebody help me!" It took 30 minutes for him to kill her. Nobody came. Was it because nobody heard her cry? It would be nice to think so, but the police discovered that 38 people had heard her screams. They had looked out of their windows, but nobody cared enough to come to help; nobody even bothered to call the police. When questioned later by the police, they said they didn't want to get involved.

We say to ourselves indignantly, *How hard-hearted can people be? Why those miserable miscreants! They deserve a fate far worse than that young woman.* Yet how many of us sit by daily, weekly, yearly, watching people go to a fate far worse than that which was suffered by Kitty Genovese, and we decide not to get involved? It took Kitty a half-hour to die, but there are millions who go to a place where they will never die, who go to everlasting torment. And yet we don't care enough to do anything to help them. How about your heart? Are you really concerned for the lost?

COMMANDED TO WITNESS

Jesus Christ calls every one of us to be a witness for Him. Every last person who names the name of Christ is commanded to bear witness to Christ, to proclaim the gospel to others. Whether clergy or layperson, young or old, it is the responsibility and privilege—the inestimable privilege—of each of us to be a witness for Jesus Christ. Have you been such a witness?

Some of you say, "Well, I just witness by my life. I can't talk about religion." I don't know where you ever got such an idea as that. On the cover of the *Presbyterian Journal* years ago were these words: "You can no more catch a dose of Christianity than you can catch a dose of geometry."

There is a gospel that must be proclaimed. "I declare unto you the gospel...that which I also received, how that Christ died for our sins according to the scriptures; and that he was buried, and that he rose again the third day" (1 Corinthians 15:1, 3-4).

We are commanded to bear witness to the gospel of Jesus Christ, not simply to live a nice life.

As long as we merely just try to live as nice people, then we simply bring glory to ourselves. We are called, rather, to speak His praise.

Several years ago, a friend of mine in the ministry was on the platform debating a man who was advocating a "voiceless Christianity," saying, in effect, that the important thing was that we just live our Christian lives and somehow people would catch the gospel. He said that words had no meaning.

My friend wrote the words, "Take me to Cuba," on a slip of paper and handed it to this gentleman. He suggested that when he boarded the plane to go home from the meeting, he give those four words to the stewardess. It would change his life. Everyone got the point.

We can't have faith and love and not witness for Christ. If we really believe Christ, then we will really have to witness.

Suppose you were walking down the street one night and passed by a neighbor's house. Suddenly, you saw flames pouring out of the children's bedroom window. You might say to yourself, *Now I really ought to tell my neighbor that his house is on fire. But I would sound rather strange standing here in the street shouting. People might think I'm some sort of a fanatic. Best that I just go home, get down on my knees, and pray about it.* There is not a person reading this who would do that. Rather, we would rush up to the front door and exclaim, "Fire! Fire! Your house is on fire!" Why? Because we believe those flames are real.

Jesus Christ, meek and mild, who came to save us from pain, said unbelievers shall go into everlasting torment; they shall be cast into a lake of fire.

But, unfortunately, coiled in the soul of many who profess Christianity, there is the serpent of unbelief that doesn't really believe those things. Do we really care about people?

A young lady came to see me recently. She was sobbing. I asked her what the trouble was. She said that a friend of hers was going through a very difficult time and he was in great heart pain. It hurt her so much to see him in pain that she was moved to tears. I thought, *How many of us have the same kind of admirable concern for people who are going to far greater pain than any that has ever been experienced in this world?*

William C. Burns was a young Scotsman who lived in the country. He was simply Billy Burns when he visited

Glasgow with his mother for the first time. As they were walking down its crowded streets, she noticed that her 17-year-old son, a devout and dedicated young Christian, was missing. She retraced her steps and after many anxious moments discovered him in an alley. There, about 20 feet away, he was sitting with his back against the wall, his knees up in front of him, sobbing. His Scottish mother rushed up to him and asked, "Billy, Billy, what ails you?"

I shall never forget his words: "Oh, Mither! Mither! The thud of those Christless feet on the way to hell breaks my heart."

Would to God there were people today whose hearts were broken by the thud of Christless feet on their way to a Christless eternity. Do such feet touch your heart?

Aunt Sophie was a converted scrubwoman. She didn't have much education, but she was a dear lady and her heart was filled with song. Whenever she could, she would share the love and grace of Christ. She was getting old, and one day someone made fun of her by saying that she was seen talking about the love of Christ to a wooden Indian standing in front of a cigar store.

When Sophie heard this, she replied, "Perhaps I did. My eyesight is not good. But talking about Christ to a wooden Indian is not so bad as being a wooden Christian and never talking to anybody about the Lord Jesus."

How is it with your heart?

FEAR OF WITNESSING

Many people don't witness because they are afraid. I know because there was a time in my life when I was afraid to talk to people about Christ. But I am happy to say that by the grace of God, I was enabled to overcome paralyzing fear. Today it is an inexpressible joy to be able to share the gospel with anybody, under any circumstance.

A young man recently shared with me his fear of sharing Christ. He knew he ought to be witnessing about Christ, but he was terrified at the thought. He made every excuse to keep from witnessing while all the time pretending he wanted to. While seated on a bus one day, he became really burdened in his heart about this matter and prayed, "O, Lord, if You want me to witness to somebody today, give me a sign." Of course, we don't really need a sign for God has given us His commandment in His Word. 'Ye shall be witnesses unto me," said Christ in His final declaration (Acts 1:8).

But soon a gentleman in a three-piece suit sat down next to him. No sooner had he sat down than tears began to stream down his face. The young man apprehensively glanced at him. The man's shoulders began to shake as he sobbed uncontrollably. After several minutes, he turned to the young man and said, "My life is a shambles; I don't know what to do. Oh, if I could only find God." He looked the young man right in the eye and said, "Do you know God?"

The young man prayed, "Lord, is this a sign?"

Well, do you have that kind of fear?

A HOLY BOLDNESS

God can deliver us from fear. Christ can set us free and give us boldness to witness for Him. We read: "Now when they saw the boldness of Peter and John…they marveled; and they took knowledge of them, that they had been with Jesus" (Acts 4:13).

If we would have the boldness of Christ, we need to spend time sitting at His feet, communing with Him, reading His Word, asking Him to cleanse us.

Many people don't witness because they haven't kept short accounts with God. They haven't really repented daily of their sins. They are involved in things they know are wrong. They feel that if they opened their mouths, they would be hypocrites—and so they would be. We need to repent of our sins. Many times the silence of Christians is simply a testimony to the uncleanness of their souls.

When we experience the joy of forgiveness, when our souls are washed whiter than snow and sparkle like the morning dew with the grace of God, then there will come, said C.S. Lewis, "a spontaneous overflow of praise and adoration," and we will want to share that with others.

One of the inevitable results of enjoyment and delight is to want to share it with another. "Isn't she beautiful?" "Wasn't that a magnificent sunset?" "Did you ever see such a beautiful picture?" In fact, it would hardly be fun to go into a museum and behold such magnificent art without having someone there to share it with because in sharing, we complete it. If we know the joy of daily communion with Christ, we will want, out of an overflowing heart, to share that enjoyment with others. "Out of the abundance of the heart the mouth speaketh" (Matthew 12:34, KJV).

But for many Christians, their hearts are dry and empty and there is no overflow. We need a quiet time with God.

We need to draw nigh to Him to get that fullness, that joy that only He can bring. "At thy right hand there are pleasures for evermore" (Psalm 16:11, KJV)—not following afar off. Do you have the love and concern in your heart that makes you feel you want to share the love of Christ with others?

Dwight L. Moody tells of seeing a steel engraving that pleased him very much: a picture of a cross emerging out of tumultuous waves of the sea. Clinging to that cross with both hands was a woman. Afterward, Moody saw another picture which made him look upon the first one somewhat askance. It was a picture of a person coming out of the dark water with one arm clinging to the cross; with the other, she was lifting someone else out of the waves.

A well-known hymn states it well:

Must I go, and empty handed,
Thus my dear Redeemer meet?
Must I go, and empty handed?
Must I meet my Savior so?
Not one soul with which to greet Him:
Must I empty handed go?

An elderly lady in England who was of nobility with great wealth and estates had come to the end of her life. A friend asked her why she was so despondent. She said it was because she was going to die soon. Her friend replied, "But you are a Christian and to die is gain."

"Yes, that's true," she said. "For 40 years I have been a Christian, but now I face death with the terrible awakening that I have never won a soul to Christ." A few days later, just before she died, she was heard to say, "Oh, for just one more opportunity to witness for Christ."

A CHALLENGE TO WITNESS

In a certain church not one single person had been brought to Christ in a whole year. The pastor gathered the officers together and said, " Let us make a covenant that if the Lord cannot use us to bring in some souls for Him in the near future, all of us will resign."

The next morning one of the officers went to his store with a heavy heart. He invited the first clerk that he met into his office. They had a heart-to-heart talk and soon the clerk accepted Christ. Then another and another was called in. By late afternoon, 11 people had been led to Christ. The other officers had also been busy. The following Sunday 30 men were received into the church on confession of their faith in Jesus Christ—because the officers had become genuinely concerned about the lost estate of their fellowmen.

Rowland Hill was a great preacher. He had a magnificent voice that could be heard a long way off. He would stand in the park or on a street corner and preach to multitudes. Often they would mock him and laugh at him and call him a madman. One day he said, in effect, to the crowd: "It is an interesting thing that you mock me. A few months ago when I was approaching a town, I saw a gravel pit cave in and bury three men alive. It was about one mile from town, and I knew there wasn't time enough to run back for help. I hastened to the rescue and shouted help until my voice was heard in town. No one called me a madman then."

Unfortunately, many people fear the frown of men more than the frown of God. The New Testament states, "For we cannot but speak the things which we have seen and heard" (Acts 4:20).

Someone has said, "There are two kinds of people: There are those who cannot but speak, and there are those who cannot speak."

In which group are you? It is a matter of the heart. "Out of the abundance of the heart the mouth speaketh" (Matthew 12:34, KJV).

OVERCOMING FEAR

Many people don't know how to witness; but in my church, parishioners have an opportunity to be trained to overcome their fear. God has ordained that the pastor-teachers train the people to witness. We have a training program called Evangelism Explosion that has been in existence for more than 25 years. Thousands and thousands of people have come from all over the world (and more than 100 nations) to learn how to share their faith in Christ. But there are still many who are not involved... who are not concerned...who are not witnessing...who are not learning...who are not multiplying...who are not training others.

We can change the world. We can spread the gospel across the face of the earth. But is your heart softened, malleable?

During the reign of Oliver Cromwell, lord protector of England, there was a shortage of silver coinage. Cromwell sent some soldiers to a cathedral in search of silver. They reported, "The only silver we can find is in the statues of the saints standing in the corner."

"Good!" exclaimed Cromwell. "We'll melt the saints and put them into circulation."

Would to God that we could melt the hearts of all of the saints of God and put them into circulation.

Out of a burning heart, a believing heart, and a loving heart, we would be constrained by the love of Jesus Christ to share the gospel of Christ.

God wants you to be trained to effectively, graciously, and confidently share the gospel of Jesus Christ and to multiply yourself around the world. I trust that you will want to say, "Yes, I want to be involved! I want to learn to share my faith; I want to multiply and train others; I want to become a witness for Jesus Christ; I want to turn the world upside down. I believe we can change the world."

I hope that your heart is touched and melted by Christ.

I hope that you will become a part of the greatest adventure in the entire world: the adventure of co-laboring with Jesus Christ in the transformation of the world. Everything else in this world is of minor significance by comparison.

We can change the world.

> *D. James Kennedy, Ph.D., is senior minister of the nearly 10,000-member Coral Ridge Presbyterian Church in Fort Lauderdale, Florida. He is founder and president of Evangelism Explosion International. He is chancellor of Knox Theological Seminary; founder of The Center for Christian Statesmanship in Washington, D.C., which endeavors to bring the gospel of Christ to those in government. He is founder of The Center for Reclaiming America which seeks to equip men and women to work in their communities to transform the culture. He is the author of more than 45 books. His messages are broadcast by television and radio throughout America and in 156 foreign countries. Kennedy is a summa cum laude graduate and holds nine degrees. He is listed in several dozen registries, including: "2,000 Outstanding Intellectuals of the 20th Century"; "International Man of the Year 1999-2000" by the International Biographical Centre, Cambridge, England; and the "1,000 Leaders of World Influence" by the American Biographical Institute.*

2

The Way of Christlikeness
JAMES I. PACKER

I am writing to Christians who want to be like Christ. Maybe you have had some sort of faith in Jesus for many years, or maybe you committed yourself to Him only yesterday. The point is that now you are really serious about being His follower. You know that He, the person whose life on earth is described the Gospels and explained in the Epistles and who reveals himself from His throne in the Book of Revelation, is for real. He has drawn you to himself and made you realize that henceforth you must be totally His. You trust in Him as your Savior, your Lord, you God, your Friend, your Hope, and the lover of your soul. You know He died for you on the cross and then rose and returned to heaven where now He reigns. And you know that one day He will come for you to take you into His glory. You know He has introduced you into His Father's family where He is the eternal Son and you are an adopted child, "ransomed, healed, restored, forgiven" as one hymn puts it. And you know that the Father and the Son together have sent the Holy Spirit into your heart to renew and transform you.

So you know that much of what you have been has to change. There is need of repentance which means a change of mind and attitude that leads to changes in conduct. There is need of self-denial which means saying no to your instinct to put yourself first so you can say yes to the summons to put the Lord first. And because you never reach the end of your self-centeredness while you are in this world, your repentance and self-denial will have to be repeated as long as life lasts.

Also, there has to be ongoing trust in the love, faithfulness, and wisdom of the divine team—the Father, the Son, and the Holy Spirit—the three persons of the Trinity who are working together to bring you to heaven's glory. Our triune God has a plan for your present holiness and future happiness that goes beyond anything you can imagine at this moment.

Your part is to rearrange your life so as to bring joy to Jesus and honor to your heavenly Father and to reassure yourself that God knows what He is doing with you, whatever difficulties He allows to come your way.

Already you know, deep down, that working to please your Lord rather than yourself brings more inner peace and joy than anything else you can ever do. Praising and serving God and spreading the good news of Jesus and His love is the way of life that your heart longs to pursue.

Have you recognized yourself in what I have said? If so, I can put in a nutshell the point I have been making: By God's grace you are now Jesus' disciple, which means pupil; and the lesson you must learn and practice for the rest of your life is to be Jesus-like. That is where I hope this chapter will help you.

And who am I to be addressing you like this? I am an old pastor who is also a college professor. I have been a believer since I was 18, and I have been writing pastoral books for more than 40 years. I think Jesus Christ, God incarnate, is the most wonderful person; and the Bible, the written Word of God, is the most wonderful book that this world has ever seen. Since some people fancy Christian writers and professors are a race apart, not like ordinary citizens, I often introduce myself to audiences by telling them I am just one more sinner saved by grace. In this chapter I shall not say anything that I do not myself believe and try to live by. I am sharing what I think I know. The reason I think I know it is that I found it in the Bible, and I discover that real Christians have been on this track for 2,000 years.

So you and I are not alone.

THE SUMMONS TO CHRISTLIKENESS

Every religion has its own ideal of behavior, but the ideals are not all the same just as the gods worshipped are not the same. The God of the Bible, the Triune Creator, is holy: The Father is holy (John 17:11); the Son is holy (John 6:69); the Spirit is holy (John 14:26). This word covers everything that sets God in contrast with us, His creatures; but the heart of the meaning is moral purity and perfection. When God brought the Israelites out of Egypt to Mount Sinai, He told them through Moses that He was their God who wanted them as His "treasured possession...a kingdom of priests and a holy nation" (Exodus 19: 5-6, NIV). Then to set the standard for their holiness, He gave them the Ten Commandments (Exodus 20: 1-17). These state in negative form the positive ideals by which all God's servants in every age should live: revering God himself (commandments one to four) and relating to others in a way that shows proper respect and good will and so honors the God who made them and values them (commandments six through ten). It was this pattern of holiness that Jesus summarized when, asked which was the greatest commandment in the Law, He replied:

> *"'Love the Lord your God with all your heart and with all your soul and with all your mind.' This is the first and greatest commandment. And the second is like it: 'Love your neighbor as yourself.' All the Law and the Prophets hang on these two commandments"* (Matthew 22:37-40).

So love, according to Jesus, is the true heart of Christian holiness.

Though Jesus was not selecting from the Ten Commandments, as His questioner no doubt expected Him to do, He was quoting the Old Testament. His first commandment is in Deuteronomy 6:5 and His second in Leviticus 19:18. "Love" is His key word. What did He mean by it here? That loving God includes praise, thanksgiving, prayer, obedience, loyalty, testimony, avoidance of sin, and aiming to please God in every life activity is clear from Jesus' own story. He said, "I love the Father and...do exactly what my Father has commanded me," and "I always do what pleases him" (John 14:31; 8:29). We also see this in His life as the Gospels record all the expressions of devotion to and fellowship with the Father that I listed above.

If you want to know what love of God means in practice, then watch Jesus. As for what He meant by loving one's neighbor, this becomes clear in His story of the Good Samaritan, told in response to the question, "Who is my neighbor?" Our neighbor, Jesus teaches, is anyone with whom we have any contact at all. From family, friends, and people with whom we work and worship to our most casual acquaintances and those we bump into as the Samaritan bumped into the half-dead Jew in the gutter. And love to our neighbor means doing all we can to help at his or her point of need.

We sometimes meet the notion that law and love are opposed, but that is not so. The Bible view, rather, is that law, prescriptive and restrictive in the standards it sets, is love's eyes while love, self-denying and self-giving for someone else's good, is law's heart.

Paul interpreted the mind of Christ with precision when he told the Christians at Rome: "Let no debt remain outstanding, except the continuing debt to love one another, for he who loves his fellow man has fulfilled the law. The commandments, 'Do not commit adultery,' 'Do not murder,' 'Do not steal,' 'Do not covet,' and whatever other commandment there may be, are summed up in this one rule: 'Love your neighbor as yourself.' Love does no harm to its neighbor. Therefore love is the fulfillment for the law" (Romans 13:8-10).

As we naturally love and look after ourselves and seek our own interests, so we must learn supernaturally to love others and under the guidance of the law of God to seek their best interests. It is very clear and very demanding.

What does Jesus mean when He says that the law and the prophets—that is, the Old Testament teaching on the moral and spiritual standards of a holy life—all hang on this law of love? He means that God's law touches motives, purposes, and attitudes of the heart as well as actions. And that God, who searches our hearts as well as observing our actions, calls for right inward motivation as well as right outward performance. That where there is no desire to exalt and honor God out of grateful affection and to advance others' wellbeing out of real good will toward them, holiness is out of one's reach, whatever one does. Proper motives as well as proper performances (and, we may add, proper dependence on the Holy Spirit) are needed for genuine holiness—a point that the Pharisees never grasped despite Jesus' attempts to make it clear to them.

Holiness also involves an ongoing quest to realize and enjoy more of God's fellowship than we are conscious of at the present moment.

Longing to enjoy God is a big part of holiness, as the Psalms show.

To pull the threads together: Law-keeping in love, honoring God, and helping people are what practical holiness amounts to. To this all Christians are called; Jesus, our incarnate Lord and Master, is both our mentor and our model. His job, within the frame of holiness as defined, was to "give his life as a ransom for many" (Mark 10:45). Our job, within that same frame, is to follow His example by loving God and people in the thoroughgoing way that He did, giving ourselves in service in whatever way each life situation, judged by Scripture, proves to require of us. Our heavenly Father wants to see in us the family likeness that reflects His own perfection, and that from all eternity appears already in the beloved Son who is His image (see Colossians 1:13-15). Christlikeness, then, is the life and destiny to which we are called.

The New Testament is explicit in showing us that imitating Christ—"following" Him by the way we live— is a proper description of our discipleship. "Follow my example, as I follow the example of Christ," urges Paul (1 Corinthians 11:1). "Your attitude should be the same as that of Christ Jesus" (Philippians 2:5). And Jesus himself, having performed the servant's task of washing the disciples' feet, tells them: "Now that I, your Lord and Teacher, have washed your feet, you also should wash one another's feet. I have set you an example that you should do as I have done for you" (John 13:14-15). C.S. Lewis expresses the thought by saying we should act as little Christs to each other. Our calling is precisely to "follow in his steps" (1 Peter 2:21).

THE SOURCE OF CHRISTLIKENESS

Our business as Christians is to live like Christ. But how? Is it just a matter of willpower and self-discipline as keeping the Scout law is said to be? Or is something further involved? To answer this we must first be clear on what happened at the time we came to faith.

"If anyone is in Christ, he is a new creation," wrote Paul (2 Corinthians 5:17). That is literally true.

The divine power that made the world and ourselves has united us as believers to the risen Lord in such a way that our inner being, the core of our identity and the source of our personal energy which Scripture calls our "heart," is now utterly different from what it was before.

Teachers used to say that if raising Jesus was the greatest miracle, then the renewing of our hearts in Christ comes next. Previously our heart was sin-shaped so that at the deepest level we were self-centered and anti-God in everything. But now our heart is Christ-shaped so that our deepest desire matches that which eternally drives the Son of God—namely, to love and serve and please and honor and exalt and glorify the Father. In us this desire becomes a longing (almost an instinct) to uplift and glorify all three persons of the Trinity together.

Paul speaks of this heart-renewing re-creation as dying and being raised with Christ (see Romans 6:1-14) and views it as the first step toward God's total transformation of us, body and soul, into the image of the Son which is the final goal of grace in our lives. The apostle John, echoing Jesus, calls this inner remaking of us, new birth, brought about by the Holy Spirit (see John 3:1-16). Paul states the gospel as a call to accept this remaking. "You were taught, with regard to your former way of life, to put off your old self, which is being corrupted by its deceitful desires; to be made new in the attitude of your minds; and to put on the new self, created to be like God in true righteousness and holiness" (Ephesians 4:22-24). John pinpoints trust in the risen Savior for salvation and the actual practice of love and righteousness as the sign of being born again (1 John 2:29; 3:9; 4:7; 5:1-4). And both Paul and John, with Jesus, affirm that the Holy Spirit now indwells believers to sustain them in the living of their new life and to carry on in them the work of character transformation (sanctification, we call it) as they continue with Christ (see John 14:16-17; Romans 8:9-11; 1 John 3:23; 4:13). Paul pictures Christian living thus: "Where the Spirit of the Lord is, there is freedom [freedom, that is, from sin's bondage]. And we, who with unveiled faces all reflect the Lord's glory, are being transformed into his likeness with ever-increasing glory, which comes from the Lord, who is the Spirit" (2 Corinthians 3:17-18). Paul's point, I think, is that we become like what we look at, so our eyes should be on Jesus constantly. Such is the Christian's new, supernatural life, viewed as if were from the inside in terms of the divine dynamic that produces it.

In light of all this, we see how to answer the question, How many we live like Christ?

First, we must be clear that for born-again believers, Christlike living is no more or no less than being *natural*—doing what we most want to do because of the way our hearts have been changed. Obeying and pleasing God, along with praising Him, are now our meat and drink. Christians who misbehave not only grieve the indwelling Holy Spirit (Ephesians 4:30) and with Him the Father and the Son, but they also make themselves miserable by doing violence to their own new nature and acting in a way that, deep down, they do not want to.

Second, we must be clear that external pressures and allurements (the world), internal pressures and allurements (the flesh or indwelling sin, meaning our unregenerate, anti-God inclinations and habits), and the personal grandmaster of temptation (the devil) all oppose our new life of holiness so that there is a constant battle to be fought for obedience and self-denial and purity of heart and life and Christian love for other people. In this battle, four words are key.

WATCH

Be on guard. Suspect yourself. Look to your Lord to alert you to approaching danger and strengthen you for the struggle when temptation comes.

PRAY

Admit to God and yourself that you are weak and ask for strength to fight till you win in each moral and spiritual combat as Jesus himself fought and won. Don't think that, alone and unaided, you can resist the down-drag of sin within you. You can't. Ask for help. It has been said that "Help!" is the best prayer anyone ever makes. Brood often on Jesus' words to the sleeping disciples in Gethsemane (Matthew 26:41).

STAND

Plant your feet. Stand steady, saying no to the devil and resisting his suggestions till he withdraws—as he will. This is spiritual warfare (Ephesians 6:13-14), and God's provision, put to service, will bring victory. God's promise is: "Resist the devil, and he will flee from you" (James 4:7).

MORTIFY

"Put to death," or simply "kill," is what this ancient word means. What we must aim to kill is sin still active in our moral and spiritual system (Romans 8:13; Colossians 3:5). We are to starve our sinful cravings, challenge our sinful habits, and build defenses against both not only by praying for divine help but also by enlisting prayerful help from others. Making ourselves accountable to fellow Christians is often the crucial move in combating persistent sin.

It helps in this to keep your eyes on Jesus, asking yourself how He would act in your situation and asking Him to stand by you and keep you from failing Him in this or any aspect of your discipleship.

Third, we must remember that in the battle for obedience throughout our Christian life, "it is God who works in you to will and to act according to his good purpose" (Philippians 2:13). So when we are able, or rather are enabled, to do anything right, we should thank God for it and not dream of taking the credit to ourselves.

THE SHAPE OF CHRISTLIKENESS

It only remains to beg you, as a growing Christian, to be realistic in recognizing that the Christlike life is not a bed of roses. Christians today, I find, will not stop assuming that as disciples of Jesus Christ, they will be shielded from what Shakespeare's Hamlet called "the slings and arrows of outrageous fortune." But they are wrong. The mistake has unhappy consequences for when things go wrong—loss of loved ones, loss of money, loss of job, loss of health, or whatever—they conclude God has let them down, and their discipleship is sometimes dreadfully damaged as a result of thinking so. So I want to be very up-front about this before I sign off. Look at 1 Peter 2:20-24: "If you suffer for doing good and you endure it, this is commendable before God. To this you were called, because Christ suffered for you, leaving you an example, that you should follow in his steps. 'He committed no sin, and no deceit was found in his mouth' [Isaiah 53:9]. When they hurled their insults at him, he did not retaliate; when he suffered, he made no threats. Instead, he entrusted himself to him who judges justly. He himself bore our sins in his body on the tree, so that we might die to sins and live for righteousness; by his wounds you have been healed."

Here is *suffering*, the agony of the cross; *submission*, the uncomplaining endurance of undeserved ill-treatment; *self-denial* and *self-control*, in maintaining silence in face of abuse and doing no more than committing himself to God the Father whose will He was doing; and *service*, the redeeming of us by bearing our sins.

If we are to be Christlike in serving others and if we are to accept our heavenly Father's discipline for our growth in holiness (see Hebrews 12:1-14), we must expect troubles—and troubles of a kind that we would not have had were we not believers.

My very last word to you, as a growing Christian, is: Get into the Psalms—by which I mean, let the Psalms get into you. The Psalter is a God-given book, and Jesus used it. We gain immeasurably by doing the same. It took me more than 10 years to get into the Psalms, chiefly because I fell so far short of the psalmists' passion to know God and get close to Him in all life situations and in all religious activities. I am very anxious that you should not repeat my failure. The passion for God—for His communion and fellowship, for His glory and His praise—must be the biggest thing and the central thing in every Christian's life. You cannot have Christlike holiness, the holiness of Jesus' "first and greatest" commandment, without it. None of us should ever allow ourselves to forget that.

James I. Packer, D.Phil., was born and educated in England. After ordination, he served several churches and Christian institutions of higher learning. In 1979, he become professor of Systematic and Historical Theology at Regent College, Vancouver British Columbia, where in 1989 he was installed as the first Sangwoo Youtong Chee Professor of Theology. In 1996 he became Board of Governors' Professor of Theology. Married with three children, Packer has preached and lectured widely in Great Britain and America and is a frequent contributor to theological periodicals. He is the author of numerous books, including one of the bestselling evangelical devotional books of all time, Knowing God. *He is an executive editor and visiting scholar of* Christianity Today. *He is also general editor of the English Standard Version of the Bible published in 2001.*

3

The High Cost of Discipleship

STEPHEN F. OLFORD

Please read Luke 9:57-62; 14:25-35.

The mandate of our risen Lord is to "make disciples of all the nations" (Matthew 28:19, NKJV). The full implications of that imperative are spelled out in the teaching ministry of Jesus. This partly explains why the word *disciple* occurs more than 200 times in the Gospels alone. This is not so much a verbal observation as it is a moral indication of the kind of person that Jesus Christ calls to follow Him in life, service, and death.

The word *disciple* comes from the Latin *discipulus* which is derived from the verb *discere*, meaning "to learn." The Greek word *mathetes* denotes "one who follows both teacher and teaching." The disciple must have teachability, stickability, and useability under the enabling power of the Holy Spirit.

In the two passages selected for this chapter, the high cost of discipleship is both extrapolated and illustrated. With anointed eyes and abandoned hearts, let us consider the words of Jesus.

"Great multitudes" were traveling with the Master. He knew by their enthusiasm that they wanted to be healed, fed, or saved from Roman domination. The fact is that the multitudes were expecting the wrong things of Him. And He turned and said, "If anyone comes to Me" (Luke 14:26).

The conditions He laid down are:

NO RIVALS

"If anyone comes to Me and does not hate his father and mother, wife and children, brothers and sisters, yes, and his own life also, he cannot be My disciple" (14:26). Discipleship means giving one's first loyalty to the Lord Jesus Christ; anything less is virtual treason if Jesus is truly Lord. There is no other response than full submission to His sovereignty. This is the primary explanation of the Master's use of the word "hate." There is no place in Jesus' teaching for literal hatred of people.

There is, however, a deeper meaning here. Jesus is making a distinction between redemptive love (which is divine) and possessive love (which is human).

If our relationship to our nearest and dearest does not flow out of redemptive love, it will not last. Possessive love is basically selfish and therefore doomed to failure. When Jesus Christ is unrivaled in our lives, then we love Him first, and the overflow of that love reaches out to family, friends, and even foes. But Jesus must be unrivaled.

We may have fathers, mothers, and spouses, and enjoy their loving attention, but they cannot rival the Lord Jesus. We may have children and enjoy their loving submission, but they cannot rival the Lord Jesus. We may have brothers and sisters and enjoy their loving communion, but they cannot rival the Lord Jesus. We may have self-lives and enjoy their lofty ambitions, but they cannot rival the Lord Jesus.

God has declared that "in all things [Christ must] have the preeminence" (Colossians 1:18). Can we, therefore, give Him less? A thousand times no. For in doing so we reveal that we have a rival in our lives. Discipleship demands that Christ should reign unrivaled in our lives, having preeminence in our thinking, speaking, and acting.

We need to pray:

> Jesus, Thy boundless love to me
> No thought can reach, no tongue declare;
> Then [bend] my wayward heart to Thee,
> And reign without a rival there.
>
> *Paul Gerhardt*

NO REFUSAL

"And whoever does not bear his cross and come after Me cannot be My disciple" (Luke 14:27). The disciples had often seen criminals take up their crosses and proceed to their execution so the disciples knew what cross-bearing meant. For one thing, it was a one-way journey; those men never came back. Taking up the cross means ultimate self-denial.

In 1937, Dietrich Bonhoeffer gave the church his book, *The Cost of Discipleship.* It was a masterful and powerful attack on "easy Christianity" and "cheap grace." Perhaps the most poignant words in the entire volume are, "When Christ calls a man, he bids him come and die."[1]

This is the path the Master trod,
Should not the servant tread it still?

To understand the deeper significance of saying yes to the implications of the cross, we need to ponder what Paul has to say about the cross in our daily lives as set out in his Epistle to the Galatians.

Three verses should be studied:

Bearing the cross means dying to the principle of the old life.

"I have been *crucified* with Christ; it is no longer I who live, but Christ lives in me; and the life which I now live in the flesh I live by faith in the Son of God, who loved me and gave Himself for me" (Galatians 2:20). The old principle was, "Not Christ, but I." The new principle is, "Not I, but Christ." That is, a life with the "I" crossed out and God's will supreme in everything.

In Gethsemane, Jesus prayed, "Not My will, but Yours, be done" (Luke 22:42). In prophetic language He could affirm, "Behold, I come; in the scroll of the book it is written of me. I delight to do Your will, O my God, and Your law is within my heart" (Psalm 40:7-8). Once we have learned the application of the cross to the self-life, we have solved the problem of making the right decisions in our lives. We no longer ask, "Should we do this or go there or marry so-and-so?" The issue is not what we want to do but what is God's "good and acceptable and perfect will" for our lives (Romans 12:2).

Bearing the cross means dying to the passions of the old life.

"Those who are Christ's have crucified the flesh with its passions and desires" (Galatians 5:24). Instead of responding to the calls of the old nature, we set our affections on things above. That is, we transmute—or sublimate—those very passions, desires, and hungers that have been crucified to the higher purposes of His risen life in us.

Bearing the cross means dying to the program of the old life.

"God forbid that I should boast except in the *cross* of our Lord Jesus Christ, by whom the world has been crucified to me, and I to the world" (Galatians 6:14). The old program was, "Go *with* the world." The new program is, "Go *into* the world," no longer pandering to the world but preaching to "all the world" (Mark 16:15).

NO RETREAT

"Whoever of you does not forsake all that he has cannot be My disciple" (Luke 14:33). Forsaking all is following the Lord Jesus without retreat. This is illustrated in Luke 9:57-62. These three vignettes are recorded to help us understand the cost of following Jesus. In each case the Master made clear that forsaking all means no retreat.

No room for tentativeness.

"It happened as they journeyed on the road, that someone said to Him, 'Lord, I will follow You wherever You go.' And Jesus said to him, 'Foxes have holes and birds of the air have nests, but the Son of Man has nowhere to lay His head'" (vv. 57-58). There was nothing wrong with the way this young man offered his allegiance. The only problem was that he did not reckon with the hardships of discipleship. Jesus perceived his tentativeness. What a glimpse this is into the life of Jesus and the cost of the Incarnation.

It teaches those of us who follow the Son of Man that, while here on earth, we are not promised luxurious living or beds of ease. We are so quick to respond with enthusiasm at the outset, but are we prepared for the hard journey to the end?

The Son of God goes forth to war,
A kingly crown to gain;
His blood-red banner streams afar:
Who follows in His train?
Who best can drink his cup of woe,
Triumphant over pain,

Who patient bears his cross below,
He follows in His train.

Reginald Heber

No room for trifling.

"Then He said to another, 'Follow Me.' But he said, 'Lord, let me first go and bury my father.' Jesus said to him, 'Let the dead bury their own dead, but you go and preach the kingdom of God'" (vv. 59-60).

With a little understanding of the background, it becomes evident that this young man's father had not just died. "The Jews counted proper burial as most important. The duty of burial took precedence over the study of the Law, the temple service, the killing of the Passover sacrifice, the observance of circumcision, and the reading of the Megillah."[2]

What the young man was implying was more subtle. In effect, he was suggesting that he would gladly follow the Lord Jesus once his father was dead. Then he could enter into his inheritance and enjoy financial security in case the cause of Christ should fail.

The Master's response was sharp and searching: "Let the dead bury their own dead, but you go and preach the kingdom of God" (v. 60.) The young man was talking the language of the unregenerate, which was in direct contrast to the demands of the kingdom. Jesus could not wait for all the conveniences of the young man's self-interest.

No room for turning.

"And another also said, 'Lord, I will follow You, but let me first go and bid them farewell who are at my house.' But Jesus said to him, 'No one, having put his hand to the plow, and looking back, is fit for the kingdom of God'" (vv. 61-62). The third man, like the first, offered his services, but he interposed the condition that he must say farewell to those at home. At first sight this seems reasonable, but a closer look reveals that this young man had not cut ties with all that represented his past life.

So Jesus points out that the kingdom of God has no room for those who look back when they have their hand on the plow. With one hand on the plow and with other goading the oxen, there is only one way to go: forward.

The cause of failure in discipleship can be traced to this problem of turning back. Lot's wife retreated and became a monument to uselessness and shame (see Genesis 19:26). Jephthah would not go back and become a monument of usefulness and sacrifice (see Judges 11:35; Hebrews 11:32).

The challenge of discipleship involves our willingness to face the cost, in the light of Calvary, and then with joyful abandon to pray:

> Dear Lord, in full surrender at Thy feet,
> I make my consecration vows complete:
> My life I yield to Thee;
> Henceforward, there shall be
> No rival, no refusal, no retreat.
>
> S.F.O.

But Jesus is not finished. Just as we have looked at three vignettes to illustrate forsaking all for His name's sake, we now examine three parables Jesus gave to illustrate the cost of following Him.

The cost of building a tower.

"For which of you, intending to build a tower, does not sit down first and count the cost, whether he has enough to finish it—lest, after he has laid the foundation, and is not able to finish, all who see it begin to mock him" (Luke 14:28-29). The tower was in all probability a vineyard tower from which a watchman could see and protect his master's harvest. An unfinished tower was considered a humiliating disgrace. It was imperative, therefore, that the builder should sit down and count the cost.

There is no more humiliating disgrace than unfinished work for God. So many start with great promise, but they fail to finish in like manner. Jesus wants disciples who never give up until they can cry in triumph, "Finished!"

The cost of fighting the enemy.

"Or what king, going to make war against another king, does not sit down first and consider whether he is able with ten thousand to meet him who comes against him with twenty thousand? Or else, while the other is still a great way off, he sends a delegation and asks conditions of peace. So likewise, whoever of you does not forsake all that he has cannot be My disciple" (vv. 31-33). This second parable comes from the king at war. It is obvious from the language employed by Jesus that there is little hope that a king with 10,000 soldiers can defeat his opponent with 20,000. In such a predicament no one sits down to wait for defeat. He takes action to negotiate a peace treaty while the enemy is still "a great way off."

In the first parable a builder is free to choose to build or not to build. In this second parable, the other "king... comes against him." As A.M. Hunter observes: "In the first parable Jesus says, 'Sit down and reckon whether you can afford to follow Me.' In the second He says, 'Sit down and reckon whether you can afford to refuse My demands.'"[3]

The cost of salting the earth.

"Salt is good; but if the salt has lost its flavor, how shall it be seasoned? It is neither fit for the land nor for the dunghill, but men throw it out. He who has ears to hear, let him hear!" (vv. 34-35). Salt is a symbol of the Christian (Matthew 5:13). The question is: What kind of Christian? Is his life preventing corruption? Is his life flavoring society? Is his life fertilizing the land? To accomplish this, a disciple must be pure, potent, and penetrating. If salt is adulterated by impurities, it is good for nothing. If a disciple is not "worth his salt," whatever other qualities he may have as a disciple, he is useless. So Jesus concludes: "He who has ears to hear, let him hear!" (Luke 14:35). That is a present imperative: "Let him go on hearing."

God make us unashamed builders (see 1 Corinthians 3:9-17), undaunting fighters (Ephesians 6:10-17), and unadulterated saltpeters (literally, "salt of the rock," 1 Peter 1:13-25). This can only be actualized in us when there is no rival, no refusal, and no retreat in our lives as disciples.

Stephen F. Olford, Ph.D., is founder and senior lecturer of the Stephen Olford Center for Biblical Preaching. He is known for his expository preaching and pastoral leadership. Olford served as minister of Duke Street Baptist Church in Richmond, Surrey, England (1953-59) and Calvary Baptist Church in New York City (1959-73). He is the voice of the Encounter *radio program, a weekly 30-minute presentation heard in the United States, Canada, and overseas. He has been honored twice by National Religious Broadcasters. In 1987, he received the Distinguished Service Award in Washington, D.C., for 27 years of radio broadcasting and the NRB South Central Chapter Honor Award in 1991 for over 30 years of presentation of Christ through media. In 1980, Olford founded the Institute for Biblical Preaching to promote biblical preaching and provide practical training for ministry. He wants to see expository preaching restored to the pulpit, spiritual revival in the church, mobilized evangelism in the world, and righteousness and social justice in our nation. Olford and his wife, Heather, have two sons: Jonathan and David, both involved in Christian work.*

4

Principles of Discipleship

DAVID MOHAN

Jesus made absolutely clear that was involved in following Him. A disciple of Jesus will put His claims first regardless of the cost. A disciple is determined to follow Jesus Christ, learn from Him, and live according to His will.

We all have a survival mentality. It is natural. We are born fighters, but that natural desire to survive creates a conflict. Paul said, "I am crucified with Christ" (Galatians 2:20, KJV). That is not survival. We all want resurrection, but most of us do not want crucifixion. The desire to survive makes for mediocre living. It eats away at conviction making it too easy to compromise and next to impossible to confront.

The result of the survival mentality is spiritual stagnation— maybe not death but not exactly life either. The desire to survive creates a tendency to excuse our lack of effectiveness.

It hinders us from completely obeying God and robs us of His power and blessing. When we strive for men's approval, that's about all we will get. What we miss out on are the riches of God.

A number of Bible characters, because of selfish desire, lost the best that God had for them. Lot chose the well-watered plains of Jordan. He took what was best for himself and lost his family in the deal. Ananias and Sapphira withheld from God what was rightly His and lost their lives. King Saul wanted to keep his throne and all the glory to himself. He lost everything. All these people had this in common: They lost what they tried to keep. Whatever the self-driven individual holds tightest, he loses. It is a paradox that Jesus taught: "Whoever wants to save his life will lose it, but whoever loses his life for me will save it" (Luke 9:24, NIV).

The disciple must not have a selfish survival mentality.

The training of the 12 disciples was a priority for Jesus during the three and a half years of His public ministry. He commissioned all His followers to train other disciples in turn.

The impact that Jesus' disciples had on the world shows its value. A small number of committed disciples who have been well trained will achieve more for God than large numbers of converts who lack spiritual depth. Discipleship is God's chosen strategy to reach the world. If one disciple led just one other person to Christ and devoted a whole year to training him and the following year both discipler and disciple each made on new disciple apiece and so on each year, in about 32 years the whole world's population would be saved.

PRINCIPLES OF DISCIPLESHIP

A lot of baby Christians do not know these basic, costly principles:

1. *A disciple lives continually by the Word of Jesus.* Disciples commit themselves to follow through on the teachings

of the Master. Jesus will speak living words to us daily through the Holy Spirit. We also need to live out the commands, teachings, and example He has already given us. Discipleship is not mainly inspiration but instruction. Obedience to the Word of God is a stable foundation.

2. *A disciple commits his life completely to the Master.* Jesus has the right to demand this commitment; He laid down His life for us. Jesus is totally committed to us and He wants the same from us in return.

3. *A disciple lives in a fruit-bearing relationship with Jesus (John 15:4-5).* When a tree is so full of sap that it can no longer hold it, the result is fruit. When a Christian is full of Christ, others see Him and hear about Him and are thus spiritually reborn into the kingdom of God. New believers are fruit of discipleship.

4. *A disciple is committed to unconditional sacrificial love for others (John 13:34-35).* This is no ordinary human love which God has demonstrated toward us. It is selfless love that does not look for any return to stimulate its actions. The Greek word for this love is *agape* which means selfless love. God and others are more important than selfish desires.

5. *A disciple is dedicated to the fulfillment of the Great Commission (Matthew 28:18-20).* The goal of discipleship should be to win other disciples, not just converts. Converts may change their minds, but disciples follow their Master. In evangelistic crusades we emphasize decision-making and often forget to emphasize making disciples. That is why so many

churches are not growing. There are so many weak, baby Christians.

MATURITY

The end result of discipleship is spiritually mature Christians. Maturity does not come automatically with increase in age, knowledge, or experience but is the result of gradual spiritual growth on the basis of obedience to Christ Jesus.

Spiritual maturity leads to fruitfulness in service for God (Matthew 25:14-30); a humble willingness to serve others (John 13:12-17); a close relationship with Jesus (Galatians 2:20); the fruit of the Spirit manifest; and a consistent, holy walk before God and man.

Without spiritual maturity, there can be no true leadership— and leaders are necessary for churches to grow.

Only mature Christians will be able to effectively stand against the devil and his power of darkness. It is only the mature disciple who, through his loving example, is able to convey the character of Jesus to the world. Winning converts adds to the numbers of born-again *believers*, but discipleship makes mature reproducers who will in turn multiply the numbers of born-again *disciples*.

PAYING THE PRICE

Many Christians have settled for a form of discipleship that bears little resemblance to the teachings and expectation of Jesus.

His words are often compromised out of expediency or to avoid personal cost. As a result, many Christians fail to witness; and the church is regarded as weak, ineffective, or irrelevant. God's children are to demonstrate the life-transforming presence of Jesus in the world. Many Christians follow the worst or least effective persons. God wants us to imitate His best people and ultimately to imitate Jesus himself.

Discipleship without cost is not true discipleship. Out of love for Jesus, His disciples are willing to apply His standards to their lives, deny themselves, and take up their cross daily to follow Him. Their cross in not a burden imposed on them but something they willingly undertake for the sake of the gospel. Jesus challenged everyone to first count the cost. In view of the high cost He required, it is not surprising that He ended up with only a few deeply committed followers. But those few were enough to change the world. True discipleship will cost us all. Disciples of Jesus cannot be half-hearted in anything they do. They are to follow Jesus as He lived and died for the principles of the kingdom of God. Luke 14:25-35 is worth another look. There are three things a true disciple must deny: his people, his life, his possessions.

Denying one's own people

The Scripture says we must hate parents; wife and children (immediate family); brothers and sisters (inclusive of a wider circle of people with whom we are in contact).

What does *hate* actually mean? The Scripture tells us to honor our parents, love our brothers and sisters. Jesus loved His mother dearly; but when it came to the love of the heavenly Father, all other natural attachments went strangely dim. He loved His Father supremely. This is brought forth vividly in one of Jesus' questions: "Who is my mother, and who are my brothers?" He said, "Whoever does the will of my Father" (Matthew 12:48, 50). The love for His Father and the will of His Father were the first priority in His life. Therefore, hating parents, immediate family, brothers and sisters means that we need to sever our natural affection and attachment with them if they be a hindrance for us to love Jesus, follow Him, and to do His will.

Denying one's own life

In Jesus' day, anyone carrying the cross through the streets of Jerusalem must be a criminal telling everyone "Goodbye...I am going to die." Similarly, carrying our cross means we are going to die to the world. No more name, fame, self-will, self-life, or ego. "I have been crucified with Christ and I no longer live, but Christ" (Galatians 2:20). Taking up the cross is self-denial.

The cross that we carry has three important aspects: (1) Suffering and hardships for Christ are the lot of His disciples. You will be persecuted and some killed. (2) Every disciple becomes a foot soldier for the kingdom of God—engaging in spiritual warfare, pulling people out of the kingdom of darkness into the marvelous light through the ministry of reconciliation with the help of the Holy Spirit. (3) Discipleship calls for patient endurance—learning a life of contentment.

Denying one's own possessions

Giving up 99 percent is not enough. We should never consider anything our own. Our life, property, bank account—everything—must be given into His hands. It is only He who allows us to use them. We should have no attachment to material things. Abraham laid his son, Isaac, on the altar. All that is valuable to us must be placed on the altar before God. Strong attachments to material things nullify true discipleship.

Two parables

Jesus' parables in Luke 14 show the disciple as always building and battling. In order to build a tower, one must calculate the cost. This is talking about the Christian life. First, we must lay the foundation (Hebrews 6:1). Many receive salvation, baptism in water, even the baptism in the Holy Spirit, but they are not able to finish the race; they backslide. This is the sad condition of many: They fall away. Building a tower means building a multistoried building. If you only have a foundation, you are not able to complete the building. People will ridicule you. So you must count the cost.

Many preachers never preach about the cost of discipleship. They always preach about blessings and prosperity.

That is why we see weak Christians. We must recognize there is a price to becoming a true, mature disciple.

Another parable portrays the Christian life as battle. Before battle, you must consider the cost and strength of your army. The devil comes against the believer with a powerful army. If you are Jesus' disciple, you will be very strong to defeat the enemy. You will overcome the devil at every point of your life, just as Jesus did. If you are not a true disciple—if you are attached to your own life and property—you will never be able to overcome. Being in the army calls for total devotion, not half-hearted commitment.

Those who don't pay the cost will be like salt that has lost its flavor. It is useless; it will be thrown away. Jesus wants quality in His followers. The church needs disciples who will pay the cost for discipleship. They will be good salt with full flavor who will transform their communities.

God is calling His bride to be spotless, holy, and blameless. Christians must rise up to genuine discipleship, understand the required depth, and be willing to pay the price. In this age of technology, the church has adopted different techniques to attract people; but we must go back to the basics—the basics of discipleship for it is the only method that God has commissioned the Church to follow.

New Life Assembly of God in Chennai (formerly Madras), India, grew, then plateaued. Then God spoke to us very clearly about going back to the basics. This plan of discipleship was implemented in our church through the small-group system where evangelism, nurture, and discipleship take place.

Our Lord has blessed our church abundantly, and it has grown to be a strong congregation. I praise God for giving us a vision to make disciples. By the grace of God, we have strong and mature leaders and disciples. All glory, honor, and praise we give to our Lord and Savior.

David Mohan is an Assemblies of God minister. He committed his life to the Lord at age 21 and later was called into ministry, receiving his schooling at Southern Asia Bible College in Bangalore, India. In 1973, Mohan pioneered New Life Assembly of God in Madras (now Chennai), India. Current attendance for Sunday services is more than 18,000 in six services. Water baptism takes place twice each Sunday. Prayer is at the heart of the church's ministry—with daily prayer at 5 a.m. and a 24-hour prayer room that is never empty. New Life Assembly has started 120 branch churches and sent out 60 missionaries to India and neighboring countries. With 1,315 home-care cells and more than 60 doctors ministering to the community in the area of public health and social services, the church is continuing to grow. Mohan maintains a focus on evangelistic outreach.

5

Living in Light of the Lord's Return

GEORGE D. COPE

I awakened in a cold sweat. Jumping off my bed, I began running through the house calling my dad, mom, sister... anyone. But no one was to be found. In the most vivid dream of my young life, I watched as Jesus came for His Church. My godly parents were taken into heaven just like the last dozen evangelists had described. Even my sister, who couldn't have been that much better than I, was leaving with my parents. But why wasn't I going? Taking matters into my own hands, I began to jump heavenward. When that failed, I climbed the familiar tree in our backyard where this Technicolor scene was occurring. Reaching the highest branch, I saw my family pass by on their way into heaven. I grabbed for my dad's leg as if to catch my rightful ride but missed and started a rapid descent. The approaching impact startled me out of my dream, and I hastily ran to see if I'd truly been left behind.

Those raised in churches with a premillennial theology can easily relate to this. But rather than struggling with my past, I was strengthened—with fundamental truth that needs reintroduction today to a church that is more concerned with the here and now.

Christ's return has lost its emphasis in today's church, 20 centuries removed. The emerging first-century church believed Christ's return was imminent; we have only idealized it, lulled into the notion that Christ will not return in our lifetime. What has numbed the nerve of our prophetic conscience?

A man lay sleeping when suddenly his room filled with light, and the Savior appeared. The Lord told the man he had work for him to do and showed him a large rock. He explained that the man was to push against the rock with all his might. Day after day the man did this. He toiled many years from sunup to sundown—his shoulders set squarely against the cold, massive surface of the unmoving rock—pushing with all his might. Each night he returned home sore and worn out, feeling his whole day had been spent in vain. The adversary, seeing discouragement, placed questionable thoughts in the weary man's mind: *You've been pushing against the rock for a long time, and it hasn't budged. Why kill yourself? You are never going to move it.*

These thoughts discouraged and disheartened the man. *Why kill myself?* he thought. *I'll just give the minimum effort; that will be good enough.* But one day he decided to take his troubled thoughts to the Lord. "Lord," he said, "I have labored long and hard in Your service, putting my strength into doing what You've asked. Yet after all this time, I have not even budged that rock. What's wrong? Why am I failing?"

The Lord responded compassionately: "My friend, when I asked you to serve Me and you accepted, I told you that your task was to push against the rock with all your strength which you have done. Never once did I mention to you that I expected you to move it. Your task was to push. And now you come to Me with your strength spent, thinking that you have failed. But look at yourself. Your arms are strong and muscled, your back sinewy and brown, your hands are callused from constant pressure, and your legs have become massive and hard. Through opposition, you have grown much and your abilities now surpass those which you used to have. You haven't moved the rock—but your calling was to be obedient, exercise your faith, and trust in My wisdom. This you have done. I will now move the rock."

Do you identify? In our results-oriented society, pushing the message of Christ's imminent return has often left us spiritually spent and feeling like prophetic failures. Like Peter, we find ourselves trying to answer the scoffer's question: "Where is this 'coming' he promised?" (2 Peter 3:4, NIV). Jesus didn't give us a time or date but signs and constant reminders of His impending arrival: "Behold, I am coming soon!" (Revelation 22:7).

In light of the urgency Scripture places on our Lord's imminent return, how do Christians keep from falling prey to our fictitious friend's syndrome of failure?

In Matthew 24 and 25, Jesus recognized man's propensity to fall short of anticipating His return, so He reinforced, through parables, practical steps that would secure His followers as they worked and waited. His instructions are often missed. A closer look reveals Jesus' admonition to be the same as the directive in our earlier story: P.U.S.H.

PERPETUAL PREPAREDNESS
(Matthew 24:42-44)

Our Lord went right to the heart of the matter with this warning. "Keep watch" (v. 42) was His command. In the maddening rush of life, keeping a focused watch can be challenging. Demands crowd our lives like rush hour in Grand Central Station. The practical challenge is *how* do we keep watch.

Jesus likens His return to a thief who comes in the night. Today alarm systems are big business. In my home every door and window are monitored. But one thing is always necessary. The alarm must be set. Sadly, Christian lives are armed with all the necessary information concerning His coming, but we often forget to set the alarm. Missing that practical step negates the value of the system.

What codes have you set to protect your spiritual life? Our real enemy lurks daily, casing how well you are protected.

The unlocked door of missed daily devotions provides access to an unprotected soul. We spend time with whom and what we love.

The cracked window of willful disobedience to kingdom principles allows entrance to the soul. Jesus made clear that we always protect what we treasure.

As you continue to wait for the Lord's return, it is imperative to *push* against any action the enemy will take to enter your house. Set the alarm with a code that only Jesus know so when He arrives, He is the only one with access.

UNEXPECTED DELAYS
(Matthew 25:1-13)

Supersonic travel and advanced communications have shrunk our world. It's nothing to board a plane in Europe in the morning and participate in a meeting in America that night. Yet nothing is more frustrating than seeing the plane sit at the gate, stranded due to bad weather. Then there is the disconcerting feeling of trying to work on a laptop computer with a dying battery. Delayed flights and missed information only heighten our anxieties. Why? We've lost our ability to wait patiently. Our microwave world has cooked us into believing delay means failure.

Jesus intended the Parable of the Ten Virgins to make us think about delays. He wasn't critical of sleep but of lack of readiness when the bridegroom came. Jesus was placing emphasis on the urgency of anticipating His return.

William Barclay tells a fascinating story in his commentary on Matthew. Three devils were coming to earth to finish their apprenticeship. They were talking to Satan about their plans to tempt and ruin men.

The first said, "I will tell them there is no God."

Satan said, "That will not delude many for they know there is God."

The second said, "I will tell men that there is no hell."

Satan answered, "You will deceive no one that way; men know even now there is a hell for sin."

The third said, "I will tell men that there is no hurry."

"Go," said Satan, "and you will ruin men by the thousands."

Barclay concluded with these words: "The most dangerous of all delusions is that there is plenty of time."[1]

Just because Christ hasn't appeared yet doesn't give us an excuse to sit idly by. Rather, we must live in light of Jesus' return and His warning that "night is coming, when no one can work" (John 9:4). His delay has delivered more time to work. The harvest fields are ready, and His unexpected delays are unprecedented privileges to *push* for more harvest.

SUBDIVIDE AND SOW
(Matthew 25:14-30)

These two terms, *subdivide* and *sow*, have their heritage in farming, something Jesus reached into consistently to teach urgency concerning His coming.

The owner in this parable subdivided his riches to three of his workers. Two showed savvy with the entrusted treasure; one buried his portion. The evident truth seems simple. Success comes from subdivision. Multiplication of the estate was the owner's highest priority even though he was physically absent. Sowing was the solution, and two of three understood it. Each knew his master would return, but only two understood the master's heart and accomplished his will before he returned.

Today many have buried their talents. Rather than subdividing and sowing, they are wearied by what seems endless effort with little results.

We must not hide what God has given us that is intended for public use. We will be held accountable for what He has placed in our hearts and hands; and if we anticipate any reward, we must subdivide and sow everything we have.

Have you buried a dream or vision, time or talent, resource or resolve? Go dig it up; begin to subdivide and sow. The Savior is coming; it's an urgent hour. Be ready to *push* forward.

HUMAN RESPONSE
(Matthew 25:31-46)

I remember the first leper I ever saw. I was a young preacher on my first missions trip to Sri Lanka. A national had taken me downtown to view Sri Lanka's leading export, tea. I watched companies from around the world exchange millions of dollars; but when I left the opulent surroundings and reentered the desperate world outside, reality set in. Lying on the sidewalk like piano keys were beggars. Humanity like I had never seen—dirty and many with open sores—rubbed against my clean body. Open hands crowded my personal space expecting the American to give them something. I remember my reaction: *Get me out of here!* Many times I have wished to have that day to live over. I walked by, choosing the attitude of a pious priest over a sympathetic Samaritan. I had never been more *unlike* Jesus than I was that day.

Some would say, "Don't be so hard on yourself, George. You were young; it was your first time in a foreign country; you were just a guest." Good excuses, but Jesus wouldn't have acted like that. His words in this text are urgent and go right to the heart of humanity's need. Jesus knew that few things were more important than our human response to the needs of others while awaiting His return. What's so difficult in understanding words like *hunger, thirst, stranger, naked,* and *prison?* "What have you done for Me lately?" Jesus asks. "While you await My return, have you invested yourself in human need?" We've been so disappointed Jesus hasn't returned that we've forgotten His admonition to a waiting church: "Work till I come." Invest your life in others: feed, quench, entertain, clothe, and visit those in need. For when you do, you look most like Jesus.

As humanity crowds your world looking for eternal hope, push your way into theirs. There is where you will find purpose until He comes.

Clearly, Jesus used these four stories to warn of more than frustration, anxiety, and despondency while His followers awaited His return. He used them to bring a sense of urgency so the time wouldn't be idle but profitable. The next time you're tempted to question why our Lord hasn't returned, recognize your need to live in perpetual preparedness, expect unexpected delays, practice subdividing and sowing your talents, and always provide human response to mankind's needs.

Never has there been a greater urgency to anticipate Jesus' return than today. Our Lord expects His Church to have massive muscle, hardened hands, and healthy hearts because we've never stopped pushing for His return.

George D. Cope attended Central Bible College, Springfield, Missouri, from 1970-74 where he earned a B.A. in biblical studies. He assumed his first position at Calvary Temple, Waukegan, Illinois, as youth pastor. From 1976 until 2000, he served three congregations as senior pastor: Belmont Evangelical Church, Chicago, Illinois; Abundant Life Christian Center, Alton, Illinois; and Bethany Assembly of God, Agawam, Massachusetts. Cope was appointed president of Zion Bible Institute, Barrington, Rohde Island, in March 2000. Cope is currently working on his master's in leadership at Vanguard University, Costa Mesa, California. He and his wife, Cheryl, have been married for 29 years and have a daughter, Jessyca.

6

The Jesus Kind of Love

J. DON GEORGE

"All men will know that you are my disciples if you love one another" (John 13:35, NIV). Jesus declares that the discipleship of the believer is validated by the manifestation of his love for other believers. Love, therefore, is the badge of discipleship.

Love is a greatly misunderstood word, even in Christian circles. Because *love* is often misused and overused, the word tends to become distorted and lose its meaning. The American entertainment industry uses *love* in such a casual way that, all too often, people dilute it to mere sentimentality. Many believe love is nothing more than a feeling.

Love, however, is more than sentiment or feeling. To some, love is a license for sexual promiscuity. Jesus, however, clearly understood the meaning of love. He understood the active nature of love. For you to understand love, you must know that love is active. That's why Jesus said, "All men will know that you are my disciples if you love one another" (John 13:35).

The apostle John wrote, "Marvel not, my brethren, if the world hate you. We know that we have passed from death unto life, because we love the brethren" (1 John 3:13-14, KJV). John says you will know you are a Christian disciple if you have love for the brethren. John continues: "He that loveth not his brother abideth in death. Whosoever hateth his brother is a murderer: and ye know that no murderer hath eternal life abiding in him" (1 John 3:14-15, KJV). John also wrote, "Hereby perceive we the love of God, because he laid down his life for us: and we ought to lay down our lives for the bretheren" (v. 16).

Clearly, the Jesus model of love is a love that knows no bounds. Some might say, "I don't think I'd mind laying down my life for Jesus, but I doubt I could put my life on the line for another believer."

Nevertheless, John said, You "*ought* to lay down [your] life for the brethren. But whoso hath this world's good, and seeth his brother have need, and shutteth up his bowels of compassion from him, who dwelleth the love of God in him?" (v. 17). John implies that when you see your brother in need and do nothing to help him, it is clear that the love of God does not dwell in you. John further stated, "My little children, let us not love in word, neither in tongue; but in deed and in truth" (v. 18). John declares our love must be more than talk.

Love, therefore, is the indelible mark of identification by which the whole world will be able to recognize your discipleship.

The world will not be impressed by your religion. It will take more than a Christian television show or a beautiful religious building to convince the world. It will take a demonstration of the Jesus kind of love.

The world is often turned off by religious ceremonies. But when the world sees willingness on the part of God's people to lay down their lives for one another, their eyes will be opened to the reality of the Christian faith. The proof of Christian discipleship is an active demonstration of love. Love isn't demonstrated until it costs something. Love has no value until you give it away.

Some might say, "I'm willing to give a cup of cold water in the name of the Lord." But it's no big deal to give a cup of cold water. You can just go the refrigerator, get it, and give it. You can just stop by a convenience store, buy a little bottle of water, and give it. It is easily obtained and costs little. The Jesus kind of love is love on a higher level.

At Methodist Central Hospital in Dallas, I saw the Jesus kind of love demonstrated. About 11 years ago a doctor diagnosed a kidney disease in the body of Rebekah Mitchell, one of the young women in our church. Rebekah struggled with this disease. The health of her kidneys continued to deteriorate year after year. Several members of Rebekah's family volunteered to donate a kidney. Each possible donor, however, was rejected by the doctors.

My wife, Gwen, and I offered to donate a kidney. We too were determined to be unsuitable donors. Then my daughter, Valerie Jones, and her husband, Kerry, our executive pastor, volunteered. Valerie, a lifelong friend of Rebekah's, was found to be a near perfect match for donating a kidney. So for several months, Valerie and Rebekah went through the procedure of preparation for Valerie's healthy kidney to be transferred to Rebekah.

On a Wednesday morning at 5 a.m., Valerie and Rebekah arrived at Methodist Central Hospital in Dallas. Both were confident, filled with faith, and ready to begin the surgery. Both families met for prayer before the surgeries. Many believers joined in intercessory prayer for a successful transplant. Both surgeries were performed without difficulty or complication. Valerie's kidney was removed and placed in Rebekah's body. The moment the kidney was connected, it worked perfectly.

Valerie and Rebekah did so well that they were waving at each other from their respective beds in the recovery room. When the doctors came out to report to the families, one said, "I believe something of a supernatural nature was involved in this surgery."

Both Valerie and Rebekah continued to improve. By Friday afternoon, two days after the surgery, Valerie was ready to leave the hospital. When the nurse arrived at her room with a wheelchair, Valerie said, "I don't need a wheelchair. I walked into this hospital, and I'll walk out of this hospital." So Valerie walked out Friday afternoon, feeling fine.

Rebekah's medical and laboratory reports continue to amaze the medical community. Many months after the surgery, both Valerie and Rebekah continue to enjoy good health with no lingering negative effects. God's people prayed and God answered prayer.

There are three important things to understand about the love of God.

LOVE IS THE ESSENCE OF GOD

God's nature is love. "And we have known and believed the love that God hath to us. God is love; and he that dwelleth in love dwelleth in God, and God in him" (1 John 4:16, KJV). This is the starting point of any study of genuine love.

God's love was manifested in both the Old and New Testaments. "The Lord thy God hath chosen thee to be a special people unto himself, above all people that are upon the face of the earth. The Lord did not set His love upon you, nor choose you, because ye were more in number than any people; for ye were the fewest of all people: But because the Lord loved you" (Deuteronomy 7:6-8, KJV). God is expressing His love for Israel.

It is not based upon Israel's wealth or prestige. His covenant with Israel required Him to love her. God loves you for the same reason. God hasn't manifested His love for you because of your physical beauty or social charm. He loves you because He made a covenant to love you. In fact, God's only attitude toward you is love. God is not harsh. He is a loving Father. The nature of God is love.

LOVE IS THE DEMONSTRATION OF GOD

As believers, we mirror God's love. We sometimes sing, "Let the beauty of Jesus be seen in me." How can that be? Do you look like God? Do you talk like God? Do you sound like God? Do you always go where God goes? You begin to look like Jesus when you manifest the Jesus kind of love. The Jesus kind of love is manifested when you are willing to lay down your life for a friend or a brother in Christ.

Three Greek words are translated as love: *eros, phileo,* and *agape.*

- *Eros* has to do with physical or sexual love—physical pleasure and gratification.
- *Phileo* speaks of the love of family and friends. This is the love that expresses itself in tender affection. It's the kind of love that you customarily have for people in your church family. *Phileo* is the love you have for a longtime friend.
- *Agape* is the Jesus kind of love. It is the kind of love that is unconditional. It is love that is unilateral.
  Unconditional love states, "I love you regardless of what you do...regardless of what you say. I love you regardless of how you treat me." Unilateral love is love expressed when it's neither requested nor deserved. Unilateral love extends love before it's deserved. That is the meaning of these verses: "We love Him because He first loved us" (1 John 4:19, NKJV). "Beloved, let us love one another, for love is of God; and everyone

who loves is born of God and knows God. He who does not love does not know God, for God is love" (1 John 4:7-8, KJV). "If a man say, I love God, and hateth his brother, he is a liar: for he that loveth not his brother whom he hath seen, how can he love God whom he hath not seen? And this commandment have we from him, that he who loveth God love his brother also" (1 John 4:20-21, KJV).

We demonstrate the Jesus kind of love by our obedience. "And this is love, that we walk after his commandments" (2 John 6). God desires us to give loving obedience to His commandments. He does not desire forced or hesitant obedience but loving obedience. Love is the nature of God. Love is the demonstration of God.

LOVE IS THE LAW OF GOD

"If ye fulfil the royal law according to the scripture, Thou shalt love thy neighbor as thyself, ye do well" (James 2:8, KJV). You see a demonstration of the royal law at Calvary. At the cross are both unconditional love and unilateral love.

Jesus demonstrated this kind of love for you and me. We weren't worthy of the love of God, but Jesus knew that we needed a Savior so He gave himself as Savior for all mankind.

The attitude of Jesus when He went to the cross was, "Father forgive them; they don't know what they do." Dying between two thieves and hanging between two worlds, He prayed for forgiveness for those who crucified Him.

You may desire a love like that but not know how to possess it. You can only receive the Jesus kind of love by the power of the Holy Spirit. If you desire to manifest *agape* love, you must allow the Holy Spirit to work in you. This love cannot be purchased or mass produced. This love is not received by osmosis. Love is the product of the Spirit indwelling your life. Love is a fruit that is grown in the Spirit-filled life. Love is the first fruit of the Holy Spirit that is mentioned by Paul in his letter to Galatian Christians (Galatians 5:22).

"For God hath not given us the spirit of fear; but of power, and of love, and of a sound mind" (2 Timothy 1:7). You have been given the Spirit of love. Let the Jesus kind of love be seen in you.

J. Don George, D.D., has served both as pastor and evangelist for the past 45 years. After six years as an evangelist, he held pastorates in Plainview and Fort Worth, Texas. He has served as pastor of Calvary Temple in Irving, Texas, since 1972. George is a graduate of Wayland Bible College. He has done additional studies at Louisiana State University and the University of Texas at Arlington. He holds the doctor of divinity degree from Oral Roberts University in Tulsa, Oklahoma. George has traveled in missionary-evangelism crusade to Europe, Africa, Asia, the Middle East, and Latin America. During the past 28 years, under George's leadership, membership of Calvary Temple has grown from 60 to more than 6,500. Calvary Temple televises its morning service, Calvary Life, each Sunday. George is a member of the Irving Chamber of Commerce, the Irving Las Colinas Rotary Club, and the Irving Ministerial Association. He is past president of the latter two as well as the Greater Dallas Assemblies of God Pastors Association. George serves on the board of International Charismatic Bible Ministries, Assemblies of God Theological Seminary, and numerous other boards and committees for civic and religious organizations. He and his wife, Gwen, have three children: Valerie, Roger, and Rodney. They have four grandchildren.

7

The Secret of Successful Living

PRINCE GUNERATNAM

The Gospel of John says: "Every branch in Me that does not bear fruit He takes away; and every branch that bears fruit He prunes, that it may bear more fruit...By this My Father is glorified, that you bear much fruit; so you will be My disciples. You did not choose Me, but I chose you and appointed you that you should go and bear fruit, and that your fruit should remain, that whatever you ask the Father in My name he may give you" (John 15:2,8,16, NKJV).

Jesus desires all believers to live successful, abundant lives (John 10:10). The secret of successful living is to know who you are and your purpose for living. This was Jesus' secret of success. "Jesus knew that His hour had come that He should depart from this world to the Father....Jesus, knowing that the Father had given all things into His hands, and that He had come from God and was going to God" (John 13:1-3). Jesus knew why He came, where He came from, where He was going, and who He was. Similarly, it is vital for you as a believer to know your God-given identity. In John 15, Jesus used the picture of the branch to describe you. You are the branch and you are here to bear fruit. This is the secret to successful living—bearing fruit.

Understanding the following four facts about being a branch will help you live a successful, fruitful life.

FRUIT-BEARING BRANCH

First, the branch is dependent. It is *of* the tree and *not* the tree. You are dependent on Christ as a Christian. You must draw from His strength, abilities, and capabilities just like the branch's survival hinges on the vine. You don't live on your own.

Second, the branch has the ability to receive nutrients from the vine and the right to use what it gets. This is exactly how a Christian lives. He is described as a vessel that needs to receive. The Christian life is one of taking from Jesus. If you know how to first receive from Him, then you have the ability to give.

Third, the branch is a beneficiary. A Christian inherits all the blessings. "The God and Father of our Lord Jesus Christ...has blessed us with every spiritual blessing in the heavenly places in Christ" (Ephesians 1:3). Your inheritance is not based on merit but on your relationship with Jesus Christ. You are heir and joint-heir with Jesus.

You have the ability and power to achieve through Christ.
"I can do all things through Christ who strengthens me"
(Philippians 4:13).

"And my God shall supply all your need according to His riches in glory by Christ Jesus" (Philippians 4:19). You are the beneficiary of every blessing.

Finally, the success of the branch is from the tree. The tree gives the strength and nourishment to the branch. The apostle Paul said, "But by the grace of God I am what I am, and His grace toward me was not in vain; but I labored more abundantly than they all, yet not I, but the grace of God which was with me" (1 Corinthians 15:10). He recognized he was a branch; and when he yielded to the tree, he experienced the sufficiency of God's grace in his life.

FRUIT IDENTIFIED

The purpose of the branch is to bear fruit. A Christian who has a strong relationship with Jesus, the Vine, will bear the following fruit:

The first fruit is holiness of life. "But now having been set free from sin, and having become slaves of God, you have your fruit to holiness, and the end, everlasting life" (Romans 6:22). Holiness is the beauty and character of God displayed in our everyday life. It is a fruit because you cannot produce it on your own. If you do, you are practicing the Pharisaic kind of piety.

There are both negative and positive aspects of holiness. The negative part is to put off the old Adamic nature. "Therefore, having these promises, beloved, let us cleanse ourselves from all filthiness of the flesh and spirit, perfecting holiness in the fear of God (2 Corinthians 7:1). "But now you yourselves are to put off all these: anger, wrath, malice, blasphemy, filthy language out of your mouth. Do not lie to one another, since you have put off the old man with his deeds, and have put on the new man who is renewed in knowledge according to the image of Him who created him" (Colossians 3:8-10).

The positive part is the many things that Christians can and must do. "Therefore, as the elect of God, holy and beloved, put on tender mercies, kindness, humility, meekness, longsuffering" (Colossians 3:12).

Holiness is to the inner man what wealth is to the outer man. If holiness is found only on the outside, it is hypocrisy.

God has invested His holiness in you. It is within you to be expressed. You need to work it out and become the person God wants you to be. Be a branch and bear what the tree is capable of.

Christian character is another kind of fruit you will bear. "But the fruit of the Spirit is love, joy, peace, longsuffering, kindness, goodness, faithfulness, gentleness, self-control. Against such there is no law" (Galatians 5:22-23). If you are the branch, it is who you are and not your abilities that will establish your Christian character.

The third kind of fruit is that of sharing or giving. The uniqueness of the fruit tree is that it never gets to eat its own fruit. It gives. It cannot help but sacrifice for others. You will know how to share. "Now all who believed were together, and had all things in common, and sold their possessions and goods, and divided them among all, as anyone had need" (Acts 2:44-45). The Early Church was a giving church. No wonder the church grew rapidly. "But whoever has this world's goods, and sees his brother in need, and shuts up his heart from him, how does the love of God abide in him?" (1 John 3:17). How can you love God if you do not share His blessings? This is also a principle of being more fruitful: as God prospers you, you give. You give so you can give more.

ABIDING

The secret to bearing fruit is to abide in Jesus. "I am the vine, you are the branches. He who abides in Me, and I in him, bears much fruit; for without Me you can do nothing... By this My Father is glorified, that you bear much fruit; so you will be My disciples" (John 15:5, 8). When the branch abides, the life of the vine flows to the branch. Whatever the branch might need, the branch communicates with the vine.

It is this communion that produces the fruit. How do you abide in Christ?

Abiding is not passive. You have to yield and do! Paul said, "Therefore, my beloved, as you have always obeyed, not as in my presence only, but now much more in my absence, work out your own salvation with fear and trembling; for it is God who works in you both to will and to do for His good pleasure" (Philippians 2:12-13). As you yield, God works in you. As you obey, God works through you.

God is the potter and you are the clay. Let God do the molding. You need to live and cooperate in the providence of God.

Abiding is also prayer and meditation. The Word says, "If you abide in Me, and My words abide in you, you will ask what you desire, and it shall be done for you" (John 15:7). The better we know the Word, the better we pray. The Word of God reveals the will of God. It is taking time to read and meditate on the Word and allowing it to sink into your heart. Prayer is not only making requests but also expressing a hunger for God, giving Him the priority of your time, delighting yourself in His presence, and pouring your heart out to God. The way to abide is to mediate and to pray.

Confession is necessary in abiding. This removes any barrier to the flow from the vine to the branch. "But your iniquities have separated you from your God; and your sins have hidden His face from you, so that He will not hear" (Isaiah 59:2). Sin is a hindrance to abiding in Jesus. Sin mars your communion with God. Nobody graduates from the altar of Calvary. Asking the Father for forgiveness and cleansing will secure the way of abiding in Him.

Abiding is also expressed by obeying. "If you keep My commandments, you will abide in My love, just as I have kept My Father's commandments and abide in His love" (John 15:10). Jesus understood the importance of obedience. He knew that the secret to abiding is to obey. "My food is to do the will of Him who sent Me, and to finish His work" (John 4:34). "I can of Myself do nothing. As I hear, I judge; and My judgment is righteous, because I do not seek My own will but the will of the Father who sent Me" (John 5:30). There is a cost to obedience. Jesus gave His life to obey. "And being found in appearance as a man, He humbled Himself and became obedience to the point of death, even the death of the cross" (Philippians 2:8). "Jesus said to His disciples, 'If anyone desires to come after Me, lit him deny himself, and take up his cross, and follow Me. For whoever desires to save his life will lose it, but whoever loses his life for My sake will find it'" (Matthew 16:24-25). If you will obey, you will abide and your life will show evidence of abiding.

CHARACTER GROWTH

A believer who abides expresses God's character, the fruit of the Spirit. These are not natural fruits but supernatural. Neither are they to be mistaken with natural gifts.

These characteristics come when you are the branch that abides in Christ.
* Absence of temptation is not the fruit of abiding. It is the overcoming of the temptation that proves that you are abiding. It is the godly character that helps you overcome.

- You experience the Father's pruning. "Every branch in Me that does not bear fruit He takes away; and ever branch that bears fruit He prunes, that it may bear more fruit" (John 15:2).
- You become dependent on the Lord. You show your dependence on God when you realize you cannot do without prayer or reading His Word and waiting on Him.
- You experience God's joy. "These things I have spoken to you, that My joy may remain in you, and that your joy may be full" (John 15:11). The joy of God does not depend on others or on circumstances. The joy of the Lord is your strength. In fact, the absence of joy is one of the telltale signs of backsliding. "For the kingdom of God is not eating and drinking, but righteousness and peace and joy in the Holy Spirit" (Romans 14:17).

Will Jesus find a harvest when He comes again? Are you bearing fruit? Let love be the motive for all you do for Christ. Love God above all else. "I beseech you therefore, brethren, by the mercies of God, that you present your bodies a living sacrifice, holy, acceptable to God, which is your reasonable service. And do not be conformed to this world, but be transformed by the renewing of your mind, that you may prove what is that good and acceptable and perfect will of God" (Romans 12:1-2).

Will you let Him help you?

The Rev. Datuk Dr. Prince Guneratnam has been senior pastor of Calvary Church in Kuala Lumpur, Malaysia, since 1972. Today the church has more than 5,600 people and 22 satellite churches. Dr. Guneratnam is the founder and chairman of the Asian Institute of Ministries and the Calvary Charismatic Fellowship. He has chaired the National Evangelical Fellowship of Malaysia since 1994 and is the chairperson of the Christian

Federation of Malaysia. A graduate of Assemblies of God Theological Seminary and holder of three honorary doctorates, Pastor Guneratnam has pastored two other churches and has preached and taught extensively internationally. He has authored a book, Living as God's Treasured Possession: A Contemporary Perspective on the Ten Commandments. He is a board member of numerous organizations, including Church Growth International and the World Assemblies of God Fellowship. He served for 26 years as general superintendent of the Assemblies of God of Malaysia. In 1999, Dr. Guneratnam received a Federal Award, carrying with it the title, "Datuk," from the King of Malaysia. He has authored articles for numerous religious publications.

8

Crossing the Cultural Divide

CRAIG J. BURTON

Jesus is multicultural. The same is true of the Father and the Spirit, the gospel, the Great Commission, and heaven. God extends His offer of forgiveness to every person in every nation. Jesus proclaimed it; the Bible declares it; waves of renewal and revival through the centuries have confirmed it: Jesus is multicultural. He has crossed the divide between heaven and earth as well as every cultural divide with a message of hope. A holy God has given His best gift to save us all from our sins.

Imagine a large steel beam spanning a street from one curb to the other. If I were to offer you $100 to cross over on the steel beam, would you do it? Likely you would. It's called easy money. Now imagine that same steel beam spanning the roofs between two large office buildings, 1,000 feet in the air. A stranger is across from you again offering $100. Would you cross over? I doubt it. Would you do it for $1,000? For $10,000? How about $100,000? Now imagine a horrifying twist. This time, instead of waving cash as a reward, the stranger is holding your child and threatening to let him drop to certain death unless you cross over. Would you do it now?

This is what Jesus did for us when He crossed the divide between heaven and earth. He willingly left glory and security and became a man so He could live and die among us. He saw us as dangling children in danger of certain death without a Savior. So Jesus crossed over. And when He did, it was without regard for who we are, where we were born, or who our parents happened to be. He is no respecter of persons; our genetics and national identity make no difference to Him. He considers every person to be worth it.

Jesus is multicultural, and it follows that His Church is also multicultural. Many consider this dynamic of the multicultural church only in terms of the body of Christ worldwide; however, today in many urban centers, the nations are literally gathering to worship in churches.

Pastors and their people are crossing cultural divides with the message of the cross without having to leave their cities.

This is the theme of Peter's preaching in Acts 2:21 when, quoting the prophet Joel, he declared, "And everyone who calls on the name of the Lord will be saved" (NIV). Jesus had told the disciples that following His departure, they would have to assume the responsibility of taking the gospel beyond the familiar regions of Jerusalem and Judea to Samaria and the ends of the earth (Acts 1:8). Jesus made it clear that the good news was available to every person in every culture. Peter's first international opportunity would come on the Day of Pentecost when many nations would be gathered in Jerusalem. Following the Upper Room experience, he literally addressed the nations without leaving Jerusalem. The church was born in a context where "Jews from every nation under heaven" (Acts 2:5) could hear the gospel. Today, congregations like this still exist—churches that embrace their God-given diversity and preach and interact across cultural divides.

In the late 1960s, municipal officials announced the establishment of a planned community in the northeastern part of metropolitan Toronto, to be called Malvern. Federal policy had opened Canada's borders, resulting in a large influx of immigrants from many nations. During this time, the leadership of Scarborough Gospel Temple, a missions-minded church affiliated with the Pentecostal Assemblies of Canada, realized that Malvern represented tremendous missions potential right in their backyard. They began operating a satellite Sunday school in 1977, and a year later conducted a first morning service. Today, more than 30 nations gather at Malvern Christian Assembly every Sunday, representing both the cultural diversity of the city of Toronto and the biblical unity of the body of Christ.

My wife, Wendy, and I have had the privilege of leading this church since 1995. Our experience is certainly not unique; in fact, throughout Toronto and other Canadian urban centers, multicultural churches are the rule, not the exception.

In Acts we discover that although Peter had preached the gospel to many nations, he himself was still not fully convinced of the extent of its multicultural nature. The converts on the Day of Pentecost, though from many nations, had all been Jews. Peter maintained a Jewish bias in terms of the gospel, the extent of which was revealed in Acts 10.

Peter was in Joppa—the same place where God dealt with Jonah when he struggled with the same issue. Jonah was not willing to cross the cultural divide to preach in Nineveh, so he boarded a ship there and sailed for Tarshish in an effort to flee from the Lord (Jonah 1:3). For Jonah,

Joppa represented that place of being outside the will of God. For Peter, however, Joppa would be the place where he would find God's will. He saw heaven open and something like a large sheet let down to earth by its four corners. It contained all kinds of four-footed animals, reptiles, and birds. Then he heard Jesus tell him to "Get up, kill and eat." Peter, being a devout Jew, had always avoided eating anything considered unclean, but the Lord challenged his bias and said, "Do not call anything impure that God has made clean" (Acts 10:9-15).

Following the vision, Peter visited the home of the Roman centurion, Cornelius. When Peter heard Cornelius's testimony, including the account of his own experience with God, he better understood the meaning of his vision in Joppa. Peter now fully appreciated the opportunity the Lord was giving him to once again preach the gospel in a multicultural setting (v. 34). He also better understood that God's forgiveness was intended for all people—not only the Jews.

What a liberating moment this must have been as Peter realized, for the very first time, the meaning of Jesus' sacrifice for the sins of the world.

Peter's sermon and actions that day model three principles that helped him build a bridge between cultures. We can still use them in this 21st century.

CELEBRATING CHRISTIAN CITIZENSHIP

Believers enjoy a higher common bond than the citizenship stamped on earthly passports, a theme on which Paul expands when he describes us as citizens of heaven in Philippians 3:20. One day, believers will be gathered in

God's presence with no regard for our earthly heritage, as proud of it as we may be during this lifetime. In Cornelius's home, Peter came to a better understanding of this truth. He then knew that God had no favorites (Acts 10:34). Peter preached Christ crucified to those Gentiles to make sure that they all clearly understood the gospel. He spoke about their most basic need—forgiveness. As they received the gift of eternal life, they also received new citizenship papers. They too became citizens of heaven.

Churches will successfully cross cultural divides as they too openly celebrate their common heavenly citizenship.

This in no way diminishes cultural diversity. Rather, it enhances it as people experience firsthand the unifying love of Christ in a corporate setting. Our most meaningful times at Malvern Christian Assembly are when we celebrate our citizenship in Communion services. We proclaim Jesus' life, death, and resurrection and take time to appreciate Christian unity in spite of tremendous diversity (1 Corinthians 10:17).

I have often encouraged our congregation by saying, "We represent over 30 nations and come in all sizes, shapes, and colors, but we are all equally forgiven because of Jesus' sacrifice on Calvary." We are different but united around the one thing that matters: citizenship in heaven.

PROMOTING CHRISTIAN DISCIPLESHIP

Peter's second bridge-building principle is near the end of his sermon. Peter an the Jewish witnesses discover that the Gentiles had received God's gift of salvation and the gift of the Spirit (Acts 10:45). Immediately, Peter asked the question of his Jewish associates, "Can anyone keep these people from being baptized with water?" (Acts 10:47). No one could deny the evidence of God's grace, so Peter ordered they be baptized in the name of Jesus Christ (Acts 10:48).

Peter wanted to ensure that the new Gentile believers were serious about following Christ. People today should share this same fervency. Jesus commanded us to "make disciples of all nations, baptizing them in the name of the Father and of the Son and of the Holy Spirit" (Matthew 28:19).

Once a person accepts Christ as Savior, water baptism is the first step in discipleship. Jesus submitted to it. Luke 3:21 says that "as he was praying, heaven was opened." What a great reason for encouraging people to follow the Lord's example! Believers can experience "open heavens" as they too submit to water baptism, and they will hear the Father's voice of commendation as they walk with Him each day.

Discipleship is vital in any church, but especially in the multicultural church. New believers from various cultures and religious persuasions often bring with them unusual views or preconceived faulty interpretations of Scripture.

To maintain unity, there must be clear agreement on the things that Jesus said really matter. Issues of lesser importance will require tolerance and understanding, but we can never dilute the fundamentals. Peter wanted the Gentile converts in Caesarea to be rooted and grounded in the gospel as quickly as possible, so he ordered they be baptized in water. We should share his fervency for discipleship concerning those we lead to Christ.

EMBRACING CHRISTIAN RELATIONSHIP

There is one final principle in Acts 10. "Then they asked Peter to stay with them for a few days" (v. 48). We might miss the significance of this unless we read in the next chapter how critical the Jews were of Peter's behavior (11:3). Not only had he entered a Gentile home, but he had also stayed there and even eaten their food. The Jews accepted Peter's explanation that "God has even granted the Gentiles repentance unto life" (v. 18). In Cornelius's home, Peter had devoted quality time to embracing relationships with his new brothers in Christ.

Embracing Christian relationships is a great blessing in a multicultural church, but it can also be a great challenge.

There may be general acceptance and appreciation for diversity, but we have found at MCA that cultures tend to stick together when it comes to friendships and fellowship. Traditions, customs, even certain types of food can become the basis for fellowship, whether informal or formal, such as in small groups. We encourage openness and acceptance for all, but some of our small groups have grown exclusively by reaching out to people of similar cultural backgrounds and this has proven to serve as an effective form of evangelism.

Establishing quality relationships took time and effort for Peter; the same is true today. Relationships are the basis for everything we do in the local church. Especially in a multicultural setting, there must be patience and understanding over time to build bridges to others.

The Lord has created wonderful diversity in the body of Christ. Multicultural churches experience that diversity in distinct and dynamic ways. Once we had to travel great distances to reach the nations; now the nations are coming to us. World evangelization still requires that we send missionaries, but some churches have the nations right in their own backyards. Our mandate is still to cross the sea, but it is also to help people see the cross right here at home. The world is filled with hatred and division.

Multicultural churches are a great witness to the love and unity in the family of God. Cultural diversity and biblical unity are nothing short of a supernatural combination that demonstrates the life-changing power of the gospel.

Jesus is indeed multicultural.

Craig J. Burton has been senior pastor of Malvern Christian Assembly in Toronto, Ontario, Canada, since 1995. More than 30 nations are represented in the congregation of 1,300. Burton graduated from Eastern Pentecostal Bible College, Peterborough, Ontario, in 1989, as well as Trent University, Peterborough, in 1984 with a B.A. in political science and economics. He worked in the banking industry for six years prior to entering full-time ministry. Burton and his wife, Wendy, have three children: Laura, Scott, and Emily.

9

Living at the Speed of Blur

MICHAEL GOLDSMITH

He awakened early, long before the first rays of light pierced the darkness. Rubbing the residue of sleep from his eyes, he shook off the weariness brought on by yesterday's events. Yesterday, what a day that had been. The day started at 4 a.m. with an important conference involving key associates. Beginning at 8 a.m., an emotionally confrontational situation consumed a number of hours. Around 3 p.m., he and members of his executive leadership team gathered at one of their homes. What was supposed to be a peaceful respite turned into further meetings. Sixteen hours into his day...nearly 8 p.m....his occupational demands pressed him for one final conference. The day had begun early and ended late. Exhausted, he dropped into bed, knowing that tomorrow's agenda was equally pressing. Apparently, he was another casualty of living at the speed of blur. One non-negotiable priority in his life prevented him from becoming entangled in the web of busyness—prayer.

The next day's agenda pressed him to rise even earlier. Dressing appropriately, he left his house and found a quiet place for solitude; reflection; personal orientation; and most important, prayer. Prayer was his key to maintaining the demands of life. The demands of yesterday had been consuming and draining. The demands of today were also potentially exhausting. He chose to pray in order to prevent the tyranny of the urgent from becoming master of his soul. Although he was a highly visible chief executive maintaining a grueling schedule, he understood and valued the spiritual core of his heart.

That chief executive was Jesus Christ. The preceding events are a modern paraphrase of Mark 1. Jesus was able to achieve focus, mission, and significance without succumbing to slavery to people, activities, and the calendar because of His commitment to spiritual disciplines.

How are we to serve Jesus Christ when activity, achievement, and opportunity fight incessantly against the spiritual disciplines necessary to transform us into His image?

Modern technology and advances are not making our lives simpler but increasingly complex. When one would expect the opposite, life is becoming tougher, more demanding, more unbalanced, and less relational.

In times of stress, expectations of others, and calendar objectives, I have often reflected on the following illustration:

A college professor begins his lecture with a large glass jar. First, the jar is filled with rocks. The professor asks the class whether or not the jar is full. Their response is yes. He then shakes the jar and adds gravel until, again, the jar is filled. He questions further, "Is the jar full?" The class answers in the affirmative. He pours sand into the jar showing that it is not filled. Now the class begins to catch on. Finally, water is poured in until at last the jar, brimming with rocks, gravel, sand, and water, is indeed completely filled.

"What is the point?" he quizzes.

One student asserts, "You can always squeeze in a little more if you try." Many would answer that way, if not verbally, then certainly in the way we choose to live.

But the reply of the wise professor is, "No, the point is that if you don't put the priorities in first (the rocks), then you will never squeeze them in later."[1]

Jesus understood this important principle of *focus.*

We can agree on two fundamental presuppositions. First, no one of greater importance than Jesus ever walked on the face of the earth. His agenda—to seek and to save that which was lost—is the ultimate priority of all of life. We never sense Jesus was in a hurry or too busy or under pressure and time-management anxiety. Second, Jesus, in His humanity, was like us. "For we do not have a high priest who cannot sympathize with our weaknesses," Hebrews 4:15 asserts, "but one who has been tempted in all things as we are [including time pressures], yet without sin" (NASV). We may think the words "all things" relate only to spiritual issues, but they also focus on personal expectations, busyness, and calendar crowding. Jesus is our example for maintaining focus in our daily affairs.

While Jesus did not have the "advantages" of our modern technology, He understood and practiced universal, transcendent principles for living at the speed of focus. Mark permits us to see the life of Jesus as an example of focused living. Here are five principles Jesus used that we can apply to our lives as we walk as His disciples.

PURPOSE

First, Jesus *established His purpose in life.* In Mark 10:35-40, James and John request that Jesus grant them positions of greatness in His kingdom—specifically to sit at His right and left hands. Jesus perceives they possess the world's "I'm number one" mentality instead of the kingdom of God's emphasis on servanthood.

Jesus speaks to them about the importance of servanthood: "You know that those who are recognized as rulers of the Gentiles lord it over them; and their great men exercise authority over them. But it is not so among you, but whoever wishes to become great among you shall be your servant" (vv. 42-43).

Jesus clinches it in verse 45 by stating, "For even the Son of Man did not come to be served, but to serve, and to give His life a ransom for many."

Jesus established the practical dimensions of His life and taught His disciples the same by emphasizing servanthood. We lose our focus and allow our schedules to be crowded to capacity because we misunderstand the priority of servanthood. Our busyness is often the result of wanting to "lord it over" someone or something instead of choosing to be servants in the kingdom of God. Jesus didn't come to be King of things but King of kings.

The personal expectation to be at the top—best, first, smartest, or fastest—is internal. No one requires you to earn the next promotion, become the top salesperson, or possess the top job. These are self-imposed. They are the results of failing to implement the principle of servanthood in every dimension of life. Work, family, leisure, and even church life afford us the opportunity to be servants of God instead of slaves to the calendar.

AGENDA

Second, *Jesus enacted His own agenda.* Mark records a day in which Jesus had performed a number of miracles, including casting out a demon, healing Peter's mother-in-law, and an evening healing rally. The following day, as Jesus is alone in prayer, the disciples find Him, telling Him that "Everyone is looking for You" (Mark 1:37). This statement is an ego stroke. In prayer, Jesus had sensed it was time to move on to other towns. He could have fed His personal ego. He could have become intoxicated with His own importance by succumbing to the expectations of others. But He didn't. "He went" to the other cities (v. 39).

Everyone has expectations of others. Listen, and you can be made to feel important, become weighted down with the emotional baggage of others. They can convince you that their need is your calling— that no one can handle this situation better than you. By succumbing, you take on the yoke (and often the bondage) of someone else's agenda. Your precious time has become lost to others' expectations.

Jesus' choice to go to other places did not signal indifference. It was a statement of control. Jesus was demonstrating that He was in control of His time. He didn't lack compassion; He understood His mission.

Enacting your own agenda sometimes means saying no to what you want to do in order to do what you must do. It may mean saying no to others in order to say yes to God— being disciplined to stick to doing what you know is most important. It's getting the rocks in the bottle before other things fill it up.

ELIMINATING THE UNNECESSARY

Third, Jesus *eliminated the unnecessary.* Jesus arrives in Nazareth where His ministry is restricted because of lack of faith. Mark 6:5 relates, "He could do no miracle there except that He laid His hands upon a few sick people and healed them." This restriction caused Jesus to leave to minister in other towns. Jesus chose not to spend much time in this city because it lacked a great enough return. Jesus could have forced himself on the people.

He could have defended His divinity, debated the religious community, or called down fire from heaven to destroy their unbelief.

Instead, He moved on to a place of greater receptiveness where He would be more effective. Proving a point could have become more prominent than living effectively. He didn't allow that to happen.

Most people easily add to the plate of their personal agendas. We are much slower to invest the time to investigate, eliminate, or delegate the multiple items on our to-do list which are nonessential and unproductive.

BALANCE

Fourth, Jesus *embraced balance.* Not every day in the life of Jesus was like the one in Mark 1. Jesus made time for balance. "It came about that [Jesus] was reclining at [the] table in his house" (Mark 2:15). Yes, there were many days that were long, pressured, and busy; but Jesus, Son of God, Savior of the world, also made time for rest. In Mark's account, Jesus "withdrew to the sea with His disciples" (3:7), "went up to the mountain" where only the disciples could be with Him (3:13), and passed "through the grainfields on the Sabbath" (2:23). Jesus found appropriate places and times for leisure.

Many Type A, highly ambitious personalities would have run full-speed, panting for breath, through the grainfield on their way to the next activity. Not Jesus. Not the disciples. We don't have to live on high octane, fully engaged 100 percent of the time. People who live this extreme usually ruin their health, destroy their relationships, miss opportunities, and lose out on meaningful living.

Busyness can be a status symbol that causes us to overload our schedules, equating it with personal value. People often attempt to "out busy" one another.

The Bible teaches the importance of establishing a rhythm for life. We should work hard and play hard, be ambitious, but also take time to smell the roses. When climbing the ladder of true success, be sure to find time for family. Balance is the key.

SPIRITUAL OVERFLOW

Finally, Jesus *experienced times for spiritual overflow.* Jesus refused to allow the demands of life to keep Him drained. He refueled. He replenished the empty reserves physically, emotionally, spiritually, and relationally. Time and again, Jesus separated himself from everything else in order to reorient the spiritual center of His life. Following that busy day in Mark 1, He "departed to a lonely place, and was praying there" (v. 35). After feeding the 5,000 and sending the disciples to cross over to Bethsaida, Jesus "departed to the mountain to pray" (Mark 6:46). Prior to His arrest, trial, and crucifixion, Jesus took the disciples to Gethsemane and said to them, "Sit here until I have prayed" (Mark 14:32).

After the busiest day of His life, instead of choosing sleep and rest, He chose prayer. He fed 5,000 people and could walk on water, yet He never underestimated the need to pray.

Instead of planning a strategy for escape, He entered the Garden of Gethsemane to pray. Jesus kept focused by keeping His spiritual life full.

We make poor decisions when we become fatigued. Ecclesiastes 10:10 well states, "If the ax is dull and its edge unsharpened, more strength is needed" (NIV). When we operate on full (emotionally, mentally, physically, or spiritually), we are in a position to choose wisely. Regrets are often the result of decisions we make while near empty.

Living at the speed of blur isn't demanded of us. It is a choice we make. Jesus, the most important person to have ever lived, by His example and teaching, models for us a pattern of focused living.

Michael Goldsmith is senior pastor of Broken Arrow Assembly of God in Broken Arrow, Oklahoma, where he has served for the last two years. The church ministries include a large preschool and a K-5 elementary school. Goldsmith is leading the church in a multimillion-dollar relocation to 40 acres of debt-free property. Goldsmith has 17 years of ministry experience which includes nine years as a youth pastor. He served as assistant youth director for the Arkansas District and spoke at youth camps and conferences. He also pastored First Assembly of God in Siloam Springs, Arkansas, for six years during which the church more than doubled in attendance. Goldsmith is a graduate of Southwestern Assemblies of God University in Waxachachie, Texas, and is a master's of practical theology student at Oral Roberts University, Tulsa, Oklahoma. He and his wife, Debbie, have two daughters: Abby and Sarah.

10

The Integrity of the Disciple

RICHARD W. DORTCH

Each disciple of Christ makes decisions every day. How those decisions are made depends on how closely each individual follows the Jesus model of integrity. Four major barriers to this are the focus of this chapter.

ARROGANT INTEGRITY

It is admirable to value one's good reputation. But there is a subtle temptation that comes with a good name. Once our reputation grows, that distinction begins to take on a life of its own. We often come to think more highly of ourselves than is safe to do.

The Scriptures warn that this sort of pride produces the perfect setting for failure. King David returned victorious from battle and, with great presumption, looked upon another woman. One of the original 12 disciples, Peter, shared a meal with his Lord and boldly proclaimed that he would follow Him until death. Before the morning sun, Peter broke that vow. Proverbs warns, "The Lord detest all the proud of heart. Be sure of this: They will not go unpunished" (Proverbs 16:5,

NIV). James writes, "God opposes the proud but gives grace to the humble" (4:6).

A respected pastor wrote about the danger we face: "Pride tells us to go it alone; God tells us to go with Him. Pride tells us to follow our instincts; God tells us to follow Him....Pride tells us to have people focus upon us; God tells us to invite people to follow us with their eyes upon Jesus."[1]

Arrogant integrity is blind. Because I took satisfaction in what others had said about my integrity, there was a time in my life that the still, small voice that wars of danger had been drowned out by the roar of "Look what's being done for the Lord."

All followers of Jesus must guard against this subtle temptation. No one starts out with the intent to fail or disappoint others. It is for the very reason that their original intentions were good and honorable that arrogance becomes such a personal enemy.

The psalmist David said, "Lift not up your horn on high: speak not with a stiff neck" (Psalm 75:5, KJV). In other words, don't toot your own horn. Whether you are in the valley or on the mountain, the tilt of the neck should always be the same. You have to look up to see God.

God takes, and God gives away. God raises up or brings down. We are not nearly as important as we sometimes think we are. There was a time I felt my reputation would protect me. I only focused on issues that were obvious and forgot about the trivial indiscretions that were swirling around me.

It is born out of a failure to realize daily that what the Bible says about people is true of us all—our flesh is constantly seeking to fulfill itself in pride.

A haughty spirit comes before a fall. How do we guard against this dilemma?

First, we must remember that we are never more right with God than when we admit we are wrong. It is difficult to come forward and say, "I was wrong. I have sinned. Please forgive me." Integrity, however, requires completeness. I must know in my heart that I have done everything that I can do to admit my errors, acknowledge my sins, and ask for forgiveness.

Arrogant integrity is the result of pride that begins to take root in the life of someone who has earned a reputation for integrity.

Second, we all need a select group of people to whom we are accountable. This group does not have to be large or influential. They must care enough about us to tell us what we need to hear.

Integrity in its simplest forms means wholeness, completeness, entirety. Integrity means that a heart is undivided; there is no hidden agenda. Loving and honest relationships provide a haven of safety and security from arrogant integrity.

SELECTIVE INTEGRITY

Some people are good at correcting errors of others, but they don't recognize the iniquity in themselves. They practice selective integrity. When we expect and demand more of others than we deliver ourselves, we set ourselves up as little gods. Selective integrity is widespread. The follower of Christ must be the exception.

Each time we experience selective integrity, whether doing it or being harmed by it, something happens inside us. We lose respect for each other and, ultimately, ourselves.

Truth cannot be selective. That is how integrity is lost.

We all do it. When we flatter people to achieve our own purposes, we are being dishonest. Selective integrity is hypocrisy. It is saying to someone, "I sure do love you," when we know in our heart that we seldom, if ever, think of him and have never cared enough to help him.

Integrity is telling the truth—and not picking and choosing our facts. Selective integrity is doing evil and expecting good to come from it.

Using selective integrity, you can tell the truth with the intent of leaving the impression of something other than the truth you have spoken.

Selective integrity is common. While we may hold truth with passion in one area, there are other times when we wink or, worse yet, close both eyes. What can we do to guard our hearts? Here, again, an accountability group is vital. The first line of defense against selective integrity, however, is with those closest to us—spouse, children, work associates.

We must create an environment at home and at work where others sense it is all right to point out any area where they feel we are sending mixed signals. The one who ultimately loses the most in selective integrity is the one practicing it.

The benefit of a more open environment at home and at work pays a valuable dividend. When I am accountable for all of my actions, then, as Paul wrote to the Corinthians, "the power of Christ may rest upon me" (2 Corinthians 12:9).

JUDGMENTAL INTEGRITY

When a Christian begins to harshly judge the actions of others, he may simply be trying to drown his own guilt. Preachers, politicians, and the media have been accused of judgmental integrity. They decry sin in the community while carrying on a secret affair or practicing dishonesty.

Jesus asked, "How wilt thou say to thy brother, Let me pull out the mote out of thine eye; and, behold, a beam is in thine own eye?" (Matthew 7:4). The person who points a finger actually thinks that darkness is light. When we fantasize that we are something we are not, the question of our own integrity becomes an immense problem. "If we say that we have no sin, we deceive ourselves, and the truth is not in us" (1 John 1:8). Somehow we must learn to deal severely with ourselves instead of pointing fingers at others.

In our quest to straighten out the world and to correct those we target, we lose the sense of what we have become ourselves. How often have we wounded a loved one or slain an enemy by negative comments? This kind of attitude says much more about ourselves than those we judge.

A judgmental concept of integrity allows jealousy and envy into our hearts. Then, instead of healing, we inflict further injury to the wounded brother or sister.

We must always ask ourselves before jumping into a matter: *Am I attempting to slay a foe or bring help, hope, and healing?* That's a choice each of us must face. "Always leave something to build on" is the admonition I heard from a wise man.

The danger lies in the Christian's temptation to ignore his own guilt by treating others more harshly. Unresolved guilt festers in his spirit, hindering his walk with the Lord and increasing the tendency to strike out at others.

How can we guard against this?

First, there is no sin we could not commit save for the grace of God. Therefore, we must have a contrite heart that depends wholly on the Lord.

Second, keep a short account with God.

The human mind has no mechanism for handling guilt. Mental hospitals are filled with people who have attempted to resolve guilt through abuse of drugs and alcohol.

Christians often judge others harshly to soothe their own conscience. They abuse not only themselves but also others in the process.

Daily confession of sins is an acknowledgment of our need for unhindered fellowship with the Father, the kind that Jesus demonstrated. Apart from His grace, sin and the judgment of others will be our constant companions.

CONSENSUAL INTEGRITY

Do you know a fellow believer who is losing or has lost his integrity? Have you gently but firmly confronted him or her? If not, you are consenting to that sin. When your heart tells you to do something—to reach out to someone who is failing—do it as quickly as possible. Don't consent to the failure. If your heart is pure, you will not consent to things that are displeasing to your heavenly Father.

It's easy to become too busy and insensitive to what our heart is saying. It takes courage to move into someone's life and speak in a loving, firm way.

People are harmed by consensual integrity. The truth *does* make a difference regardless of who chooses to look the other way. When those we trust choose to ignore truth, the results can be devastating.

Many people might retreat cowardly from being a whistleblower by quoting the Lord's admonition, "If any one of you is without sin, let him be the first to throw a stone" (John 8:7, NIV). But Jesus was speaking to a crowd that had gathered for a one-sided lynching—not to a group sincerely investigating the truth. To the contrary, the Scripture admonishes us that to choose not to do what is right is a sin of omission; and such failure is serious.

Consensual integrity is tolerated for one reason— selfishness. I don't want to get involved because it might cost me something.

The Scriptures call for us to be men and women of integrity. We must never lie or hide. The price is too great.

Consensual integrity is born out of an individual's own bent for self-preservation. The cost of going against the popular consensus for the moment can appear frightening. No one understands this better than Jesus. His message of redemption ran counter to both the religious and secular culture of His day. We must follow Him. How can we do this?

First, like Jesus, we must cultivate a passion for the Lord's will rather than our own. It begins with the question, "Given this same set of circumstances, what would Jesus do?"

That question, made popular in Charles Sheldon's classic book *In His Steps,* carries great weight. By asking it before you act and by searching Scripture for the answer, you will usually make the right decision. Ultimately, we resist the lure of consensual integrity, not by our own strength but by the power of the Holy Spirit.

Remember Peter's failure on the night Jesus was arrested? He went along with the crowd and denied knowing the Lord. Yet in Acts 4, Peter stood before the council and, under threat of his life, proclaimed Jesus as Lord. What made the difference? "Then Peter, filled with the Holy Spirit, said" (Acts 4:8). Ultimately our dependency, day by day and moment by moment, upon the Holy Spirit is our only sure defense against consensual integrity. As we take the sinner's place, He empowers us to follow Jesus—faithfully.

The traps of arrogant integrity, selective integrity, judgmental integrity, and consensual integrity lie in wait on roads on which Christ would not lead us.

When we follow Jesus, our integrity will be genuine—and Christlike.

Richard W. Dortch is president and founder of Life Challenge, Inc., an agency caring for people in crisis. For ten years he was the host of the nationally syndicated television program, You and Me. *As a pastor and missionary, Dortch helped establish Emmanuel Bible Institute in Belgium and served as its president. He was an executive presbyter of the Assemblies of God and superintendent of the Illinois District. He has served or is serving on the boards of Assemblies of God Theological Seminary; North Central University; Central Bible College; and Church Growth International in Seoul, South Korea, with David Yonggi Cho. He was chairman of the board of Evangel University. He founded several radio stations in Illinois and served as senior executive vice president, then president, of PTL. He presently also serves as an evangelist in the U.S. and overseas. He received his theological training at North Central University in Minneapolis, Minnesota, and received a doctor of divinity degree in 1979. He and his wife, Mildred, live in Clearwater, Florida.*

11

Humility: Making Ourselves Nothing

DARIUS JOHNSTON

"Do nothing out of selfish ambition or vain conceit, but in humility consider others better than yourselves. Each of you should look not only to your own interests, but also to the interests of others.

"Your attitude should be the same as that of Christ Jesus: Who, being in very nature God, did not consider equality with God something to be grasped, but made himself nothing, taking the very nature of a servant, being made in human likeness. And being found in appearance as a man, he humbled himself and became obedient to death— even death on a cross! Therefore God exalted him to the highest place and gave him the name that is above every name, that at the name of Jesus every knee should bow, in heaven and on earth and under the earth, and every tongue confess that Jesus Christ is Lord, to the glory of God the Father" (Philippians 2:3-11, NIV).

A young minister was invited to give his first sermon. After many years of study, he felt more than adequately prepared and accepted the invitation gladly. When the moment arrived, he walked proudly to the pulpit with his head held high, radiating self-confidence. But he stumbled reading the Scriptures and then lost his train of thought halfway through the message. He began to panic, so he did the safest thing. He quickly ended the message, prayed, and walked dejectedly from the pulpit, his head down, his self-assurance gone.

Later, one of the godly elders whispered to the embarrassed young man, "If you had gone up to the pulpit the way you came down, you might have come down the way you went up."

With His life, Jesus taught us tremendous lessons about humility. Paul tells us in Philippians 2 that Jesus made himself nothing.

Jesus chose not to cling to the outer expression of His divinity. He refused to parade His superiority. Instead He taught, "The Son of Man did not come to be served, but to serve, and to give his life as a ransom for many" (Matthew 20:28).

SERVANT

Jesus made himself nothing by becoming a servant. Jesus demonstrated this in John 13. The disciples had come to eat the Passover meal, and there was no servant to wash the disciples' feet. Jesus went over to the corner, took off His outer robe, clothed himself in a towel, took a basin of water, and began to wash their dirty, smelly feet. I can only imagine the awkward silence that filled the room when the disciples became aware of what Jesus was doing. Peter broke the silence by refusing to let Jesus wash his feet. Jesus assured him this was part of God's plan so Peter relented. The silence must have been thick as Jesus finished all 12 disciples—including Judas—and returned to the table.

Then Jesus asked: "Do you understand what I have done for you?" (v. 12). Deathly silence. So Jesus answered His own question: "I have set you an example that you should do as I have done for you" (v. 15).

When I first read that passage, I thought Jesus was saying we should be washing feet. In fact, every New Year's Eve our church had a foot-washing service. But Jesus did not tell us to do what He did but to do as He did. Jesus isn't asking me to run around taking off everyone's shoes and socks so I can pour water on their feet. He is asking me to make myself a servant—to touch people's lives and meet their needs.

Jesus was not after position. He was the Master...they were students.

Can I willfully serve those who may appear to be inferior or below me on some ladder of social importance?

Jesus was not after recognition. Our ego will sometimes use humility as a means of self-promotion. Jesus never practiced this philosophy. There was no award for washing feet.

Am I willing to serve without expectation of recognition?

Jesus was totally secure in who He was. The key to Christ's ability to wash feet is: "Jesus knew that the Father had put all things under his power, and that he had come from God and was returning to God" (v. 3).

Jesus understood where He came from, where He was going, and what He had. That's a good formula for overcoming insecurity—understand that our worth has come from our heavenly Father, that we are going to spend eternity with Him, and that He has entrusted us with His authority.

With that sense of understanding, we can be free to wash feet.

JEALOUSY

Jesus made himself nothing by refusing jealousy. In Mark 9, we get an insight into Jesus' view on competition. The account begins with one of the disciples a little concerned that someone is cutting in on their operation. There is a person who is not one of the chosen who is going around casting out demons in the name of Jesus. John decides that this could hurt their ministry growth plan, so he tells the man to stop. Obviously feeling good about his decision, John informs Jesus that he had taken care of this fellow who was doing such a horrible thing.

Much to John's surprise, Jesus does not give him an award of merit but a rebuke. Jesus says, "Do not stop him" (Mark 9:39). Jesus was thrilled that the kingdom of darkness was losing and the kingdom of heaven was advancing.

Maybe John should have remembered the Old Testament story of Eldad and Medad. They started prophesying in the camp, and Joshua asked Moses to forbid them. Moses said he would be glad for everyone to prophesy and refused to stop them. (See Numbers 11:26-29).

Here's the test for you: Do I rejoice when others are blessed?

A few years ago I struggled with this question when a pastor in my area was experiencing tremendous growth. I was working hard, and this new kid on the block was blowing everything away. His church was twice the size of mine in less than two years—I had been working for five years. Then God told me I had to start praying for this brother to be blessed even more. I wanted to pray for him, but not for blessing. I disagreed with his philosophy and many of his approaches. It took months for me to be able to honestly pray for God to bless this fellow pastor. The lesson was painful but effective. When I learned to honestly rejoice in his growth, God began to bless our work as well.

The war with jealousy is never won—there are always new battlefronts. That's why I must keep a daily prayer closet. Humility and jealousy can never coexist.

JUDGING

Jesus made himself nothing by refusing to be judgmental. As I study the life of Jesus, I see that one of the ways He demonstrated His humility was by refusing to judge others. Jesus said of himself, "I pass judgment on no one" (John 8:15).

This is illustrated in John 8 when men interrupted Jesus' teaching by bringing in a woman who the religious leaders said was caught in the act of adultery. Case closed; she deserves to die. It is right there in the law. What do you say?

No reply. Jesus writes in the sand.

"Come on, Jesus. What do you say? What should we do with someone caught in the obvious act of sin?"

Jesus speaks. "If any one of you is without sin, let him be the first to throw a stone at her" (v. 7). Jesus goes back to sand writing.

Interrogation over. Awkward exit of accusers.

Jesus stands. Looks around. Looks at the woman. Speaks. "Woman, where are they?" They are gone. "Then neither do I condemn you!"

In heaven someday I hope to speak with this woman. I would love to know what happened with the rest of her life.

Another illustration of Jesus' refusal to judge is in Luke 9:51-56. Jesus and the disciples are on their way to Jerusalem. Jesus sends some to a Samaritan village to get things prepared. The people of the village refuse to welcome them. James and John are indignant and ask permission to call down fire from heaven to destroy this village that would reject Jesus. Jesus rebukes James and John and simply goes to another village.

There have been occasions in my ministry when I knew that vengeance belongs to God, but I wanted to be His hand extended. There were people who were saying things and doing things and needed to be set straight. I felt I should be the one. But God hasn't yet released me to be His spiritual enforcer.

Humility means I don't have to correct everyone.

TRUSTING

Jesus made himself nothing by trusting the Father's timing. A quick journey back to Philippians 2 reminds us that Jesus humbled himself and become obedient to death; then God highly exalted Him. Travel with me to the cross. Suspended between heaven and earth is the Son of God. Unjustly tried and sentenced, He is brutally pinned to the wood by three nails. His body is ripped, beaten, and torn. Each breath is a painful struggle. He gathers enough strength for one last statement, "Father, into your hands I commit my spirit" (Luke 23:46). And then it is over.

The key word is *commit*. According to *Strong's Bible Dictionary*, the word can be translated "to deposit as a trust or for protection." Jesus was saying to the Father, "I deposit myself as a trust for You to protect." Jesus chose to trust the Father with the outcome.

Self-ego often wants to help God out when it seems that nobody notices our sacrifice, service, or efforts. Yet Jesus showed us that true humility can trust God for the outcome.

One day many years ago I sat in a cafeteria with my father sharing some unpleasant news. I will never forget his words: "Darius, your number one job is to keep *your* heart right with God. God will take care of who is right or wrong." I was learning that day to trust God's timing. This is a lesson I continue to learn.

Have you learned to humble yourself before God and trust His timing in your life?

In an age when everyone seems to demand his or her rights, the life of Jesus provides a dramatic contrast. Even the Church has been invaded by the mentality of position, privilege, and power. Servanthood seems archaic. It is time to return to Christ's example—lay down our robes of pride, jealousy, and prejudice. Then we can learn to trust God with the outcome. The world is waiting to see Jesus through us.

Darius Johnston has been senior pastor of Christ Church Assembly of God, Fort Worth, Texas, since 1986. The growing congregation relocated to their 64,000-square-foot ministry center in fall 2000. Johnston served as youth pastor at Calvary Temple, Irving, Texas, and traveled as an evangelist. Johnston is a graduate of Southwestern Assemblies of God University, Waxahachie, Texas. He and his wife, Cindy, have two boys: Brock and Brendon.

12

Living Courageously for Christ
RANDY VALIMONT

Most people define courage as an act of heroism. If that is all it is, then there is not a lot of courage in this world. We are sadly short of acts of heroism. Courage is indeed heroism, but it is also much more than that. Courage is the inner strength to stand or act when it may cost us something such as our reputations, the acceptance of others, or even our lives. As a disciple of Christ, we are called, even demanded, to be courageous.

One great example of courage is found in Daniel 3:8-25. The story of the three Hebrew men, Shadrach, Meshach, and Abed-nego, is a familiar one. These three demonstrated courage at every level.

In examining this passage, we find there are three characteristics of courage that occur repeatedly in the Bible. These characteristics must be found in the life of every believer who wants to walk and live courageously for Christ.

MINGLED WITH FAITH

The first characteristic of Christlike courage is that it must be mingled with faith. Daniel 3 chronicles the faith of the three Hebrews while they were in the fiery furnace.

They never would have made it into the furnace if they were not already men of extraordinary courage. When the first musical instrument sounded, signaling everyone to bow to the golden image, the three men stood their ground. That is courage mingled with faith. It took courage to stand, but it was faith in a cause that gave them the strength to act in civil disobedience.

Never has the world seen such rapid change and the church is a part of that change. We must be careful not to bow to any social or political influence that would compromise our faith.

In the United Sates, we have a wonderful heritage of forefathers who stood courageously for their faith. Oftentimes, when reading America's history, I marvel at the courage and faith of those early pioneers. That kind of faith and character has been exhibited around the world as men and women have risked their lives for the cause of the gospel. In Scripture, when great courage is displayed, it is always motivated by faith in a cause. As New Testament disciples, we must be motivated by the cause of the gospel.

The apostle Paul was so motivated by the cause of Christ, so filled with courage, that he penned these words under the inspiration of the Holy Spirit: "According to my earnest expectation and my hope, that in nothing I shall be ashamed, but that with all boldness, as always, so now also Christ shall be magnified in my body, whether it be by life, or by death. For to me to live is Christ, and to die is gain" (Philippians 1:20-21, KJV).

We live in a day when more than 100,000 Christians are killed every year for their faith in Christ. Believers must have faith mingled with courage. Anytime a believer has courageously stood his or her ground, especially when facing martyrdom, the Church and the cause of Christ have supernaturally been advanced. This was exemplified in the Columbine High School shooting in Colorado. A teenage girl by the name of Cassie Bernall stood her ground courageously. It was reported that when asked by one of the teenaged gunman, "Do you believe in God?" her affirmative answer was rewarded with a fatal bullet. Subsequently, her funeral was broadcast nationwide on CNN, and she reached more with the gospel in her death than in her life. Even today, faith must be mingled with courage.

MODELED BY A TEACHER

The second characteristic of courageous faith is that it must be modeled by a teacher. Shadrach, Meshach, and Abed-nego had this done for them through their friend and mentor, Daniel. Daniel started by refusing to eat the king's delicacies because he did not want to "defile himself" (Daniel 1:8). The three Hebrews saw God honor Daniel through his courageous stand. In Daniel 2, Nebuchadnezzar has a dream that he wants interpreted. The problem is that the king does not want to tell anyone the dream for fear his advisors will simply create an interpretation. He thus instructs his astrologers, magicians, and wise men to tell him what the dream was. When they cannot, Nebuchadnezzar orders all his wise men killed, along with the astrologers and magicians.

At this point, Daniel steps in and asks to see the king. He tells the king what his dream was and also gives the godly interpretation. The events in Daniel 3 would never have happened had Daniel not modeled courage in chapters 1 and 2. That is why we must be courageous. We never know who is watching us and the influence we are having.

When I was a young man, my pastor modeled courage for me. The year was 1977, and our church was growing. My pastor had an 8-year-old daughter who was afflicted with a cancerous tumor on the side of her face. For a full year his little girl fought cancer and ultimately died. During this ordeal, as an 18-year-old college student, I went to the church every workday and prayed from 8-9 a.m. Day after day my pastor slipped into the church and prayed out loud for his daughter's healing and deliverance. I don't think he ever knew I was kneeling in the pews in the back of the auditorium. He displayed such courage and faith. Many times since then, I have drawn strength from those prayers when facing my own difficulties. Courage become a way of life for me after I saw it modeled by my pastor.

Today, God has entrusted me with the responsibility of pastoring a large church with more than 100 employees. I need courage every day.

It sometimes surprises me when people say, "Pastor, that took courage to preach," or "Pastor, that was a courageous decision." You see, my mentor modeled courage and faith, and it became the yardstick by which to measure my own courage and faith.

The church today must have men and women who model courageous faith and thus encourage people to follow their example. Whether facing marital, financial, or physical difficulties, Christians must model courage and draw strength from Jesus' words in Matthew 28:20: "teaching them to observe all things whatsoever I have commanded you: and, lo, I am with you always, even unto the end of the world."

MANIFESTED BY THE STUDENT

The final characteristic of courage is when it is manifested by the student. Scholars debate why Daniel was not mentioned in Daniel 3. Most believe he must have been away doing the king's business when the call came to bow before the golden image. This apparently was the first time the three Hebrews would have to stand without their mentor, Daniel, being present. The manner in which they stood against the most powerful king of that time has inspired millions of believers through the ages.

If you ever want to be truly inspired by the courage of saints in the last 2,000 years, then read *Foxe's Book of Martyrs*. Story after story details men and women from around the world standing for their faith and the impact it had on others. Jesus said the student is not greater than the teacher. No one in the history of the kingdom suffered like our Lord. It is not too much then for us to be bold and courageous for Christ.

Several years ago, my administrative assistant gave me a framed poem for my birthday. The words inside the frame were written by a young pastor in Zimbabwe, Africa, before being martyred for his faith in Jesus Christ. I try to read these words at least once a week, and I close this chapter with these thoughts. The title of the poem is "Treasure":

I'm part of the fellowship of the unashamed. I have the Holy Spirit power. The die has been cast. I have stepped over the line. The decision has been made—I'm a disciple of His. I won't look back, let up, slow down, back away, or be still. My past is redeemed; my present makes sense; my future is secure. I'm finished and done with low living, sight walking, smooth knees, colorless dreams, tamed visions, worldly talk, cheap giving, and dwarfed goals.

I no longer need preeminence, prosperity, position, promotions, plaudits, or popularity. I don't have to be right, first, tops, recognized, praised, regarded, or rewarded. I now live by faith, lean in His presence, walk by patience, am uplifted by prayer, and I labor with power.

My face is set, my gait is fast, my goal is heaven, my road is narrow, my way rough, my companions are few, my Guide reliable, my mission clear. I cannot be bought, compromised, detoured, lured away, turned back, deluded, or delayed. I will not flinch in the face of sacrifice, hesitate in the presence of the enemy, pander at the pool of popularity, or meander in the maze of mediocrity.

I won't give up, shut up, let up, until I have stayed up, stored up, prayed up, paid up, and preached up for the cause of Christ. I am a disciple of Jesus. I must go till He comes, give till I drop, preach till all know, and work till He stops me. And, when He come for His own, He will have no problem recognizing me... my banner will be clear!

May we all have such a testimony when we face our Redeemer.

Randy Valimont has been pastoral ministry since graduation from Southeastern College of the Assemblies of God in Lakeland, Florida, in 1981. He has been the senior pastor of First Assembly of God, Griffin, Georgia, since 1993. Attendance has grown from 400 to over 2,400 on Sunday mornings, and more than 13,000 people have found Christ. Missions giving reached more than one million dollars in 2000. First Assembly is home to two academies, a daycare, a Master's Commission, and a television ministry. Valimont serves as chairman of the Board of Regents of the CIS Bible Schools and national Blind Ministries of the Assemblies of God. He also serves on numerous boards for ministry, media, and missions organizations. He serves the Georgia District as executive presbyter. He and his wife, Jelly, have been married for 20 years and have three daughters: Jordan, Danielle, and Alayna.

13

Serving Jesus and People

CLYDE C. MILLER

Servanthood is not for sissies.

Servanthood is not about hanging out with losers or grimacing while washing dirty feet or hobnobbing with politicians in showcase soup kitchens.

Servanthood is more...much more.

It seems natural for the weak to serve the dominant. We live in a world that idolizes, advertises, and visualizes the briefcase lifestyle of the decisive CEO. We see the slicks of men and women with the sky-in-the-eye, world-at-their-feet mentality on their way up. Surely such would wonder, *Who wants to be a servant?*

At best, these money magnets would intone, "Find a need and meet it" (as a way to succeed). But their motive is not to meet the need of the needy but to feed the greed of the greedy; they care not about building a better mouse trap so much as to having the world beat a path to their door.

Servanthood that circles back to self is not servanthood at all; it is pseudo-serving. Sadly, such concepts have crept into the souls of many who construct the core values of congregations.

For instance, an ambitious pastor asks, "How can I grow a church?" The question intensifies as he reads the Christian glossies that give mega-ink to mega-churches. For some of these, the cross has been reduced to a convenient Christian emblem, a golden amulet, a decoration for a soaring steeple serving as a landmark for a successful congregation.

What if the cover were ripped from their plans, dreams, and staff conferences? Would we see planning that has simply transferred the success mood from corporate Babylon to the sacred sanctuary? Would we see the CEO mentality, though robed as a man of the cloth?

Again the question is asked, "Who wants to be a servant anyway?" On the wind of the Spirit comes this trumpeted answer: Jesus does.

Servanthood is not for sissies.

Let's explore servanthood, Jesus-style, through three observations: First, only the strong can serve sincerely by choice. Second, only the truly wise can understand the value of servanthood. Third, only those who are tuned to Jesus can serve for the right reason.

THE CHOICE

Only the strong can serve sincerely by choice. Self-denial is the least popular dictum of discipleship. But servanthood, Jesus-style, enlists only those who will deny themselves, take up their cross, and follow Him (Matthew 16:24). How many men and women lavish talents on small congregations, talents that could command five- and six-figure incomes in Secular-ville? Yes, that's self-denial. In denying their right to receive their own market value in order to serve, they have denied themselves and are crucified with Christ.

True servants serve because they choose to serve. It's not just seeing a need and attempting to meet it, but it's the Good

Samaritan *seeing the needy.* He lifts the beaten and battered one onto his own donkey, takes him to the hospital, and then promises the selected caregiver, "I'll be back." The Samaritan was not simply interested in a statistic for his annual report or a good story for next month's mailer but rather in the soothed, saved, stricken soul—*and he'll be back to check on him.*

The servant does not serve from a posture of weakness or because the better ministry postions have been denied him. He takes his strength and dispenses it to the weak, the fallen, the guest, the newcomer, or the alien—the marginalized. Because he knows he has it to give, he knows he should—and because he knows he should, he does.

No, servanthood is not for sissies.

THE VALUE

Only the truly wise can understand the value of servanthood. Can you dream of a world where each person is concerned about the needs of others as much as he or she about his or her own needs? In a world like that, the nations could truly beat their swords into plowshares. The Golden Rule is at the heart of kingdom building.

Several years ago, Doug Wead wrote of the Protestant/Catholic conflict among Christians in Ireland. He observed this mind-set: "Tonight, they killed a Protestant. Tomorrow, we'll kill a Catholic." True servanthood finds a way to turn the other cheek, to be a shock absorber, not a shock.

Servants, Jesus-style, seek not simply to appease but to see, really see, the true need behind the action and find a way to meet that need.

Seen through this window, however dingy, every man or woman has equal standing; the other guy deserves life, help, and health as much as I do. And why not serve him or her with no other motivation than the fact of his or her need and my ability to meet it?

The wise know that when they raise the water level, they raise everything in the water. Helping to tutor the underprivileged child of a working, single mother raises the quality of life for all. Yes, the reward cycles back to me; I benefit, but that is not my motive.

It is a wonderful law God has put into nature. "They who turn many to righteousness shall shine as the stars of heaven," the prophet Daniel promised (Daniel 12:3, paraphrased). They shine because they are full of Light, the light of the Master Servant; and that Light lifts the fallen, the orphan, and the widow. When the quality of life of these needy ones improves, so does my community. But the true servant does not often think that far ahead. The pain of the needy is immediate, so serving is first and paramount. When that pain is relieved, it is enough. All other rewards are fringe benefits, but the fringe benefits follow naturally… or should I say, supernaturally?

THE RIGHT REASON

Only those who are tuned to Jesus can serve for the right reason. Campaign promises during elections are notoriously self-serving. "Elect me and this is what I'll do for you." Translation: "I promise you this in order to get your vote." Hence the promise of servanthood beats a familiar circular route back to self.

And who among us is completely free from the guile of self-serving? Is there no way one can serve out of a truly pure heart? Jeremiah summed it up this way: "The heart is deceitful above all things, and desperately wicked: who can know it?" (Jeremiah 17:9, KJV). May our prayer be, "O, Lord of the cross, let my pride and self-serving be washed away in the blood of Him who said, '[I] did not come to be served, but to serve'" (Mark 10:45, NIV).

Then, there is what can be called shepherd vision. Jesus, the Master Servant-Leader, was looking over a multitude of Jews one day and saw them through His shepherd vision. Did He see them as shiftless opportunists following only for the loaves and fish? No. He saw them as sheep without a shepherd. They really wanted to follow, but they had leaders who had abdicated and left them wandering.

My friend, James Armpriester, left a strong financial position as an employee of a major company to raise up a church in a depressed part of Cincinnati. Why? Because of leaderless, lost, lower income families. He has built a congregation of 200 in less than four years. But he has also acquired a grant and completed a partnership with Cincinnati State College to use his church facilities to train people for whom college and career training was only a dream. When he raises their standard of living, he raises the quality of life for this whole community.

Randy Bohlender pastors Mason Spirit Life Community Church, a church that our church planted in a fast-growing suburb peopled by Boomers and Gen-Xers. He felt led to attend a conference of creative, free-spirited post-moderns who met, 30,000 strong, in an Arizona desert. These modern-day pagans were conducting a weeklong New Age-style camp meeting called Burning Man. Money was not used there. Instead, attendees bartered with one another for their needs. Thanks to the generosity of a local Christian business, Randy and five parishioners took 5,000 bottles of water to give out free in the name of Jesus and His love for these people.

Returning, Randy wrote a sermon/essay on his experiences among these sheep without a shepherd and then posted it on his church's Web site. Because of the non-condemnatory love of Jesus that flowed from Randy's message, the promoter of Burning Man subsequently picked up the sermon/essay and added a link to Randy's Web site to a newsletter she published. Forty-five days later, Randy reported 25,000 hits on his own Web site from 20 different countries. True servanthood makes a difference.

Serventhood is not for sissies.

Steve Sjogren came to Cincinnati 17 years ago to establish a congregation of John Wimber's fledgling Vineyard churches. I really doubted his California concept would fly in this conservative area; but God gave Steve the vision of servant evangelism, what he calls "committing small random act of kindness in great ways," truly seeking to serve those who are seeking. Today, the Central Vineyard Church sees more than 5,000 people in four weekend services. One of the most innovative random acts of kindness Steve commits is to go into an area and offer to clean the toilets of small businesses. One of those businesses happened to be porn king Larry Flynt's sex-oriented shop operated by Larry's younger brother, Jimmy. The act flabbergasted the Flynts. No, they have not shut down their store; but when Steve was severely ill following a botched gall bladder surgery, one of his hospital visitors was Jimmy Flynt. Are Larry and Jimmy needy? Oh, yes, the Shepherd thinks so.

The greatest hurdle for the Christian church is to get the average Christian Joe and Jane to sincerely seek to see all men, all women as the Master Servant-Leader, Jesus, sees them.

We then receive the call, the energy, the creativity to feed the hungry just because they are hungry. We can then care for the widow, the orphan, the struggling single parent simply because he or she is lonely and we know that loneliness hurts. Alleviating the sense of aloneness is in itself reward enough.

While it is true that we, individually, cannot save the world, it is good to remember that we are not called to save but to *minister*, which means to serve. *Jesus saves; we serve.* When our eyes are opened to the tremendous power of servanthood to change the world, one person at a time, serving then springs from a position of strength, wisdom, and right motive.

My maternal grandmother, Lydia Ruth Kirk, was a sterling example of these qualities. While proud of her 1/16th Cherokee Indian heritage, she had no more than an eighth grade education, seldom left her home, and never traveled more than a couple hundred miles away from there. But her 60 years were a life of loving, smiling, cooking, cleaning, and selflessly serving her husband and ten children who all survived to adulthood. I still remember her as the love magnet that always drew the family together. Love flowed like a river back from her children to their servant mom. To a casual observer, her cotton dresses were unimpressive, her influence and position small. But she was as pure an example of the power of servanthood as I have ever seen.

May the Spirit of Him who said, "I have come to serve," fill our churches and our hearts and become the basis of all we do. "The kingdom and the power and the glory" were not enough to hold Jesus in the heavenlies or to keep Him from coming to earth to serve. Let us follow His lead.

Clyde C. Miller is pastor emeritus of First Christian Assembly of God, Cincinnati, Ohio, where he was senior pastor for 32 years and assistant pastor for four. Miller, a graduate of Central Bible College, Springfield, Missouri, was instrumental in starting outreach at the University of Cincinnati and is currently chairman of the Ohio District Chi Alpha committee.

Cincinnati Teen Challenge which he helped found in 1972. He is assistant superintendent for the Ohio District Council of the Assemblies of God, an executive presbyter of the district, and has served on various other boards and committees, including Assemblies of God Theological Seminary and Citizens for Community Values of Cincinnati which he helped found in 1983. Miller and his wife, Anita, have three children: Debra Ferguson; Crystal Winters; and Mark Miller, assistant pastor at New Song Community Church, Cleveland, Ohio. They have two grandchildren.

14

Giving It All You've Got

S. ROBERT MADDOX

Before moving to the Chicago area, I served as the executive vice president of a bible college. Traditional Christian higher education is not only about academics. At least three things occur: professional skills are developed, character training is enhanced, and social graces are addressed. College endeavors to prepare the whole individual.

The classroom is the main arena for instruction in professional skills. Life in the dormitory and chapel services give attention to character development. Times together in the cafeteria, at community events, and dating seek to refine social graces.

Courting is an important part of college. I like the comparison of a bible college to a shoe factory—it brings in heels, repairs souls, and sends them out in pairs. The Christian campus environment is ideal for finding a mate for life.

The courtship process can awaken some powerful passions. Strict rules are established for students: no walking together on campus arm in arm and no holding hands in chapel. In one of the earlier student handbooks of the college, there was even a rule against touching the other person. So couples would hold the opposite ends of a short stick instead of holding hands. Eventually, rules gave way to general principles of human contact. Rules proved ineffective when dealing with inappropriate behavior.

Students know what is right. In the classroom they are instructed in the Bible. In chapel services dynamic speakers regularly address the subject of sexual behavior. In dormitory meetings resident directors speak about campus policy.

The problem is not lack of information—the problem is doing what is right. The truth of the matter is: While in the embrace of another person, when the choice is between knowledge and passion, passion usually wins. Passion is powerful.

When it comes to being a follower of Jesus, most know that it is supposed to impact their lifestyle. Why then do lifestyles show so little difference? Jesus gave clear instructions before ascending into heaven: "make disciples" (Matthew 28:18-20, NIV). What prevents this from happening? It is not lack of knowledge; it is lack of passion. Knowledge is a tool used in the assignment, but passion is the motivation that gets the job done.

When Jesus was asked what the greatest commandment is, He responded, "'Love the Lord your God with all your heart and with all your soul and with all your mind and with all your strength.' The second is this: 'Love your neighbor as yourself.' There is no commandment greater than these" (Mark 12:30-31). He was not minimizing the need to know the Lord but understood that knowledge is not enough to keep a person serving God. There must be passion in a meaningful relationship with God—a holistic love. Once there is a deep-seated love for God, then one's passion is to excel in all human relationships. Passion is the substance and the motivation of all relationships—the people of God are to be totally in love with the Lord and with those created in His image and likeness.

The last book of the Bible records letters from Jesus to seven churches (Revelation 2, 3). The letter to Ephesus commends them for depth of knowledge—their understanding of God was seen in their deeds, their hard work, and their righteous standards. But there was on fatal flaw in this congregation—a lack of love. Through time, love had been lost. Without passion, their future was in jeopardy.

The remedy to a diminishing of love requires a willful change and a restoration of passion.

Knowledge is not enough. Jesus said, "Remember the height from which you have fallen! Repent and do the things you did at first" (Revelation 2:5).

The first four books of the New Testament reveal Jesus as a man of passion—it is a major part of His story. His passion was especially focused on people with great needs. With keen insight, He would assess problems and would bring remedy with passion.

On one occasion, Jesus had sent His disciples on a ministry assignment. They had seen wonderful things happen through their efforts. When they returned, they told Jesus exciting stories from their experiences. The crowds had become so large that there was little time to eat. Jesus decided they should get somewhere alone and rest.

When they arrived at their destination, the crowd was waiting for them. Scriptures suggest that Jesus and His disciples were weary from ministry. They were hungry and tired. But seeing the large gathering of people gave Jesus added strength. He had compassion on them and immediately began to address their needs—both spiritually and physically (Mark 6:30-44).

Jesus also had a passion against evil and sin. When entering into the temple area, He became angered by the greed and corruption there. It was not enough to simply know that the merchants' activities were wrong—their actions impassioned Him to address the problem (Mark 11:15-18).

The greatest expression of passion in Jesus is seen in the final days of His life—at the end of what is known as the Passion Week. He knew before He came what had to be done, but it was passion that made the cross a reality. When in a garden the night before, He expressed a desire to avoid the weight of sin; but His feelings for people produced the necessary willingness.

Could this be the problem with many of His followers—the lack of sacrificial passion in their ongoing relationship with God? Jesus said, "If anyone would come after me, he must deny himself and take up his cross daily and follow me" (Luke 9:23). Later He declared, "And anyone who does not carry his cross and follow me cannot be my disciple" (Luke 14:27).

To give maximum effort as Jesus did, a person must have passion. If passion is missing, then part of the solution is to get before God an ask Him to fix the "feeler" in one's life.

Like the church in Ephesus, many know what to do but they have lost the sense of God's presence and are trying to maintain momentum out of duty instead of desire.

Knowledge is not only to be understood; it is also to be felt. Knowledge is about transformation—and transformation focuses on how a person feels about life. This is often difficult for people who look at life cognitively more than experientially. When knowledge is heartfelt, it increases energy.

Here are a few actions that can help strengthen passion:

MORE PASSION BY PRESENCE

Passion is enhanced by a love that is fresh. Is regular, frequent time being given to the Lord? A marriage becomes endangered when a couple does not give time to each other. The affection necessary to sustain a strong relationship is crucial for a great marriage. The standards of this day and age demonstrate that knowing marital vows will not keep a marriage intact. A healthy marriage requires ample amounts of time devoted to intimacy.

In the same way, a meaningful relationship with God involves time in His presence through Scripture, meditation, and prayer.

The Bible is also referred to as a love letter. It reveals a God who has a passionate love for people. A person can easily forget how much God loves the world when measuring only by what is seen every day.

God's love can be questioned when evaluated by the cruelty, corruption, and calamities of life. The Bible makes it very clear that God indeed cares about all these sorrows.

Meditation is a component that is often neglected when endeavoring to gain passion. To meditate is to ponder, to reflect, and to bring clarity of thought. In the busyness of life, this activity is easily neglected. Meditation is a bridge between God speaking to His people and His people loving their God.

Communicating with God is another important part of having freshness in a relationship with Him. What His people think is important to Him. Articulating feelings enhances intimacy.

Praying that increases passion also involves heart-to-heart as well as head-to-head communication. Heart-to-heart praying is referred to in the Bible as praying in the Spirit (1 Corinthians 14:14). The Holy Spirit speaks to our heart things that are important to Him. This increases a passionate approach to life and ministry.

MORE PASSION BY PEOPLE

I worked with a leading evangelist for a few wonderful years. Shortly after being invited to join his team, I went to his home for a meeting. We went for a ride in his car in order to talk—it was the only way to get him away from the phone. I was glad he chose to do most of the talking. I was seeking a better understanding of his heart. I wanted to know what excited him, what motivated him, what gave him his extraordinary energy.

We came upon a stalled vehicle. There was steam coming from the truck's radiator. The evangelist stopped and asked if he could help. He then went out of his way to get some coolant. While helping to fill the radiator, he talked to the man about Jesus. I discovered a man who lived to reach the unsaved; it was the all-consuming fire of his soul.

Working with him changed my life. It produced a personal passion to fulfill the mandate to tell others about Jesus whenever there was opportunity. Passion in others can intensify passion in our own life.

Seek out passionate people, and it will increase your own passion. Regularly look for opportunities to be with people who are experiencing dynamic results from their efforts.

Exposing your life to their passion increases the passion quotient in you.

MORE PASSION BY PURPOSE

Passion can be misplaced when focus becomes lost. A pastor I know uses a phase that has now become a part of my own vocabulary: "It's not about us; it's about them." When purpose is mislaid, a feeling of "when is it going to be my turn?" often develops. Priorities quickly become altered and passion becomes weakened.

It becomes extremely difficult to lose passion when there is a clear focus of what it means to be eternally separated from God. William Booth, the founder of the Salvation Army, preferred that his soldiers keep before them a vision of hell more then a vision of heaven. Feeling the eternal destiny of the destitute lends itself better to creating maximum effort.

When Jesus spoke of hell, He spoke of how it felt. He created word pictures of the anguished cries of friends and relatives (Luke 16:20-31).

The subject of hell could very well be tender to you. Has someone you know died without deciding to become a follower of Jesus? Think of them. Let purpose impassion you to keep others from this horrible place.

Summer bible camps and winter retreats are terrific experiences for students. For a brief of time, young people's lives become uncluttered by television and other time-fillers. Attention is given to eternal issues. What is accomplished in events like these? Greater knowledge of Scripture? More is required than a camp or a retreat to greatly increase someone's insight of the Bible. These times are devoted to passion. When the young people get back home and into the arms of their parents, the buzz of activity is declaring that "feelers" have been fixed. Passion has been restored to their lives.

There is value in going to an event designed to rejuvenate the person who is weary and worn. Getting into a special environment when nerves are fragile is important. This can bring healing and restoration. Maximum effort, however, requires staying close to God and regularly tapping into the power of His passion.

One of the greatest models of giving your best is the apostle Paul. His word to us on this subject is this: "Whatever you do, work at it with all your heart, as working for the Lord" (Colossians 3:23).

As a 21st-century believer, living like Jesus will require great passion.

S. Robert Maddox was born and raised in Seattle, Washington. He received his education at Northwest College of the Assemblies of God, Kirkland, Washington; and Southwest State University, Marshall, Minnesota. He has served as a pastor in Montana, South Dakota, and Minnesota. Prior to coming to the Chicago area, he served as executive vice president of Trinity Bible College, Ellendale, North Dakota. Presently he is pastor of the Stone Church in Palos Heights, Illinois, and serves as the executive presbyter of the Illinois District of the Assemblies of God. He and his wife, Brenda, have four grown children and one grandchild.

15

Jesus, Example for the Home

SAM FARINA

A rooster saw a plate of scrambled eggs pass by. He turned to his wife, the hen, and said, "There go our kids—all mixed up."

In reality, many homes *have* become scrambled. The husband, wife, and children do not understand their roles or fulfill their responsibilities. And many do not understand Christ's teachings regarding marital and family relationships.

In his letter to the Ephesians, the apostle Paul presents five truths from Christ's life that should guide our actions and attitudes in the home.

TAKING RESPONSIBILITY

Ephesians 5:22-23 says, "Wives, submit to your husbands as to the Lord. For the husband is the head of the wife as Christ is the head of the church, his body, of which he is the Savior" (NIV). In many homes problems stem from the husband's failure to take responsibility for the success—or mess—of the home. The poor marital and spiritual condition of the family is often the result of a spiritually immature man. The man isn't serving as the spiritual leader of the home. The word "head" literally means "one who is responsible"—not one who is a tyrant or boss. It doesn't mean the husband exists to have his needs met. It means he exists to meet the needs of his wife and children.

First Corinthians 11:3 says, "The head of every man is Christ, and the head of the woman is man, and the head of Christ is God." Too many men covet the role of leadership without accepting the responsibility of leadership. When the wife is instructed in Scripture to submit to her husband, it actually means she is to look to her husband to have her needs met. In no way does it suggest she is inferior or incapable. Many women have a lot more going for them than their husbands. Submission is not inferiority. Philippians 2:5-7 says, "Your attitude should be the same as that of Christ Jesus: Who, being in very nature God...made himself nothing." God the Son and God the Father are equal, but the Son chose to look to the Father as the One responsible to meet His needs. That's the image and principle He's communicating to men today.

We are never more like Jesus than when we have a submissive spirit and never more like the devil than when we have a rebellious spirit.

Again, submission is not inferiority.

Many people perceive their marriage as a partnership. It is not a partnership; it is a team. Partnerships with equal partners make decisions with votes. Votes produce winners and losers. God never intended there to be winners or losers in the family. Husbands and wives are co-equals. The Bible's teaching that the man is the head can be compared to a football team. The quarterback calls the play in the huddle, but the quarterback gets the play from the coach. A marriage is to be a team. In the home, God is the coach. The man is the quarterback. But if he's a smart quarterback, he'll listen to his fellow players. He'll listen to his wife, his children. Good quarterbacks do not enter the huddle and say, "All right, you bums, I'm the quarterback so you'd better listen." If he does, the offensive line will most likely let the rush come through unabated and he'll soon be an injured quarterback. The "I am king" mentality has caused many wives and children to rebel, to join another team.

When a quarterback calls a play that wins the game with no time remaining on the clock, he is wise to share the praise with the entire team. But when the quarterback's play fails, he should take the blame. That's what God intended in the home. Instead, some men choose to blame their wives, kids, parents, or the church when their play fails. But quarterbacks who point fingers are missing the mark. They need to take responsibility if they expect the wife and children to look to them for safety and security. Marriage is not a partnership; it is a team. And it is important for a family to function as such.

ESTABLISHING PRIORITIES

A husband must let his wife know she is his number one priority. "Husbands, love your wives, just as Christ loved the church and gave himself up for her" (Ephesians 5:25).

She must know she is more important than her husband's job, his bank account, his mother, and even his children. Of the six billion people on this planet, a man should view his wife as the most important woman in the world. The Bible says, "A man will leave his father and mother and be united to his wife" (Mark 10:7). The wife gains security and comfort when she knows she is her husband's top priority. Children also feel more secure when their father conveys his high esteem for their mother.

GIVING PROTECTION

Ephesians 5:26-28 teaches men to protect their wives from emotional garbage: "That he might sanctify and cleanse [her] with the washing of water by the word, that he might present [her] to himself a glorious church, not having spot, or... blemish" (KJV). The word "spot" literally means dirt, trash, or refuse. It is the husband's responsibility to keep emotional trauma and trash from being dumped on the wife. Some husbands come home from work and the first words out of their mouths are, "What have you done all day? Look at this place; it looks like a dump." Instead of protecting her from the trash, the husband has violated God's Word and dumped on her.

Ephesians also says men are to present their wives without "wrinkle." Think of the word "wrinkle" as facial lines that come from emotional trauma. Robert Burns, a pastor, said to a group of women, "At age 50 you will have the face that your husband will give you." Some women's faces are developing wrinkles—not because they have been smiling and laughing but because of the pressure that is being brought into their house by the one who is supposed to shield her.

Certainly a wife wants to know her husband's hurts so she can bear the burden with him, but her wrinkles shouldn't come from criticism and abuse.

There are daily tasks that my wife handles. She writes checks, pays bills, balances the books, etc. If checks start bouncing and our account is overdrawn, it is not my duty to blame her. I gave her that authority, but I must also assume some responsibility. Ultimately, I'm to blame for mistakes. To behave in a biblical manner means refusing to dump verbal trash when something goes wrong.

PROVIDING SECURITY

A husband should make his wife feel secure. Ephesians 5:29 says, "No one ever hated his own flesh, but nourishes and cherishes it" (NASV). This tells us the kind of nurturing words a wife deserves. Before leaving work, men should occasionally call and say, "Honey, I'm coming home and I can't wait." Some men honk all the way up the driveway. They burst through the door and say, "Baby, lay it on my lips." They have learned to energize their mate. The word "nourish" means to provide nutrients. It is the man's responsibility to provide the emotional, spiritual, and psychological nutrients needed for his wife.

The word "cherish" means providing bodily warmth. Picture a hen sitting on her eggs, providing warmth and protection. A snake may approach the nest, but the hen will peck at the snake. She won't leave her eggs. She knows if she commits herself to providing warmth, the shell on those eggs will eventually break open and chick will emerge.

Dr. Clyde Narramore says a woman needs 12 hugs a day to be healthy. When your wife is at the kitchen sink, go up behind her and hug her. Let her know that no matter what your age, there is still fire in your mind, body, and soul to warm her. We need to provide emotional and bodily warmth. We need to hold our wives.

When your wife is crying and she doesn't know why and you don't know why, hold her as close as you can; let her know you'll cry with her.

That's what living like Jesus is all about at home.

TAKING INITATIVE

Husbands must take initiative. The roles of male and female in American culture are mixed up. Everyone knows, generally speaking, that men and women have different makeups. Men tend to be physically strong; women are often more gentle. Men tend to be less affectionate; women are often more sensitive. God built men and women differently so they could complement one another when they come together. But because some men are weak leaders, women have been forced to become the aggressors. This has caused confusion. Men should take the initiative to be servant leaders.

Many homes, however, are managed by a single parent. In these cases, with the Lord's help, parents are forced to serve as both mother and father. Day after day, they are heroic in their service to their children. They have learned to rely on the Lord. He makes up for not having another parent in the home. The body of Christ, the church, can play a key role in helping these families thrive.

Living like Jesus in our homes and marriages is pictured clearly in Ephesians 5:22-33. John Ortberg, in his book, The Life You Always Wanted, *writes, "Jesus brought a message that spoke to the deepest longings of the human heart to become not simply conformed to a religious subculture but transformed into 'new creatures.'"*

Song of Solomon 5 paints a picture of the man walking in the night rain. Soaking wet, he knocks on the door. From inside, his wife replies, "My feet are washed and my robe is off and I'm not getting up to help you." He pleads and keeps knocking. Finally she opens the door. To his surprise, perfume is dripping from her fingers. She hoped he would persist. She was actually getting ready for him. This is a picture of the male taking the initiative, using loving words to draw his love to him. How do we love our wives like Christ loved the Church? Revelation 3:20 says that Jesus stands at the door and knocks. He is knocking; we must also pursue our mate.

Home should be the place where the qualities of the new creature are most evident—clearly seen by those we have been commanded to love as Christ loved the Church.

Sam Farina is senior pastor at First Assembly of God in Concord, North Carolina. A dynamic communicator especially noted for his ability to challenge young people and leaders, he has traveled throughout the world. A graduate of Southwestern Assemblies of God University in Waxahachie, Texas, he serves as adjunct professor at North Central University in Minneapolis, Minnesota. Farina and his wife, Vicki, have a grown son, Tory.

16

In the School of Jesus

RONALD MADDUX

Psychologists tell us we are products of our past. While there is a great deal of truth in that, that is not the final word on who we are. There is another principle to consider—that we are formed by our future. Each person has hopes, dreams, and aspirations. Greater than that, each person has a call. Who we are and what we can accomplish are ultimately determined by our response to the call upon our lives and the task to which we have committed ourselves.

We are not called because of who we are or for what we have done—but for who we can be. The potential for our future is not determined by our past but by the power of the One who has called us, to empower and enable us for service—and success in that calling.

Mark 3:13 tells us that when Jesus called His apostles, He "called...those he wanted" (NIV). He did not call them on the basis of their past but the potential of their future. The story reports, "They came to him." They made a decision to commit to a call that would ultimately change their destiny. Jesus designated them apostles. He established an outcome-based mentorship program. They were not yet apostles, but He designated them apostles since that was the outcome goal of His mentorship. Jesus called them so "they might be with him" (v. 14). His mentorship program was one of character modeling. He called them "that he might send them out to preach." He gave them practical ministry assignments. Finally, in Jesus' outcome-based mentorship program, He established ministry goals for His mentorees: "to have authority to drive out demons" (v. 15). The end result of His mentoring program was that He developed a group of men who could function successfully in the fulfillment of their call. Their future was different from what their past seemed to foreshadow.

Mentoring is often overlooked as an important component in the development of believers—and particularly of those who will minister in service to the church. Frequently mentorship is confused with discipleship—but they are not the same. Discipleship is a product of the Great Commission: "Therefore go and make disciples of all nations" (Matthew 28:19). Mentorship is a product of the Great Commandment: "Love your neighbor as yourself" (Mark 12:31). Obedience to the Great Commission will move us to disciple people everywhere. Obedience to the Great Commandment will move us to come into a caring and nurturing (mentoring) relationship with those who need and want it. Discipleship establishes a *primary relationship*—between disciple and Christ. Mentorship establishes a *secondary relationship*—between the mentor and mentoree. Discipleship develops and strengthens a person's *vertical relationship* with God while mentorship develops and strengthens a person's *horizontal relationships* with others.

The church needs more mentors. While, in the strictest sense, the goal of a leader is to produce results, the goal of a mentor is to produce character. The object of a leader is to move people; the object of a mentor is to mold people.

Mentoring is a practice of personal development and nourishing that reaches back to ancient times. There are examples of mentoring in secular, Judaeo-Christian, and non-Judaeo-Christian religions throughout history. The Bible is filled with mentoring relationships: Eli and Samuel, Elijah and Elisha, Moses and Joshua, Barnabas and Paul, and Paul and Timothy, to name a few.

Historically there have been two training-mentoring models: the Greek model and the Hebrew model. The Greek model was more philosophical. It was oriented more toward the academic. It was more passive than experiential. The Hebrew model was more relational. The emphasis was more on the mentor than the material. Our great model is that of Jesus as portrayed in Mark 3.

It is interesting that today the Hebrew model is being adopted by the business and educational worlds as a means of better equipping student for the tasks before them— while the church has moved to the Greek model.

The church needs to return to the Hebrew-Christian model and develop leadership and character in the same way that Jesus developed the apostles and the apostles developed the Early Church.

This is especially important in a 21st-century postmodern world that puts a high premium on relationship and experience.

The mentorship program into which Jesus enrolled the apostles was outcome-based. Jesus did not merely call the apostles into a fellowship relationship but into a program that would produce specific outcomes—creating persons of spiritual character and integrity able to fulfill the ministry call upon their lives.

OUTCOME-BASED MENTORING

There are two continuums in an outcome-based mentoring program. Basically these have to do with the often-discussed issues of *being* and *doing*. The first has to do with progress in *personal growth*. The second has to do with progress in *skills* and *ministry development*. Each of these concentrates on three areas. Enhancement of personal growth focuses on character, community, and comfort. Enhancement of skills and ministry development focuses on comprehension, competence, and co-active ministry relationships.

- *Character*: The development of essential Christian qualities in the life of the mentoree.
- *Community*: The mentoree effectively assimilating into the ministry team or church.
- *Comfort*: The degree of personal confidence that the mentoree feels as they move into the ministry role to which God has called them.

These are all inner issues that ultimately come out of the strength of one's personal growth.

- *Comprehension*: Understanding one's ministry role as well as how it fits into the overall plan of God in a particular setting.
- *Competence*: The degree to which one is capable of successfully performing in ministry.
- *Co-active Ministry Relationships*: How well the mentoree can actually work within the context of a ministry team or the church.

In an outcome-based mentoring program, there are a number of stages toward the success of the relationship.

These are connecting, implementation, redefinition, departure, and reconnecting.

CONNECTING

Connecting is the establishment and initiation of the relationship and expectations of the mentoring process. In this stage, the mentor and mentoree will go over the nature of the mentoring relationship. They will discuss mutual expectations and goals, how both the mentor and mentoree will participate, and the desired outcomes. This is the time to determine the logistics of the mentorship.

The mentor and mentoree will decide when, how often, and how long they will meet together.

The format of the mentoring meetings will be chosen. These would include meeting for meals, at the church, place of work, or homes. Some mentoring sessions will be more structured; others, less so. There should be modeling events where the mentoree accompanies the mentor on ministry assignments and observes the mentor in action.

One goal for the connecting stage would be the development of a joint mission statement, specifically spelling out the agreed-upon objectives. A time of prayer, asking the Lord to bind mentor and mentoree together in love and mutual concern and for wisdom in this relationship, is highly recommended.

Mentoring takes time. It is important that the mentor and mentoree accept the challenge to commit the time necessary to maintain a successful mentorship. However, one must realistically arrange a schedule of meetings, readings, devotionals, etc., that can conveniently fit into one's schedule.

IMPLEMENTATION

Implementation is the stage at which the actual mentoring process begins, putting into motion the various aspects of mentorship that have been agreed upon. Mentor and mentoree will meet as previously arranged, following the agreed-upon format.

In the mentoring meeting, the mentor will work through their agenda of strengthening the mentoree according to the goals and objectives of the mentorship. It is assumed that the mentor has specific skills that speak to the needs of the mentoree. This is the time that the mentor performs the ministry of empowering another by sharing God-given resources. This can be accomplished by various methods: relating personal experiences, instruction, offering opportunities to perform various skills, etc.

The implementation stage is the opportunity for the mentoree to receive empowerment—to be the beneficiary of a transformational relationship. It is up to the mentoree to make the most of this mentoring experience. The mentoree should be inquisitive, seeking to be a dedicated learner.

Mentoring meetings should not be just about knowledge and skills development. A very important (perhaps the most important) aspect of the mentoring program is the development of spiritual character. This is accomplished through praying together, spiritual instruction, and mutual sharing of spiritual insights. No doubt this was at the heart of Jesus' intention when He called the apostles to "be with him."

REDEFINITION

The redefinition stage will allow the mentor and mentoree to review (early in the mentorship) how things are going, if the expectations of both mentor and mentoree are realistic, and if the mentoring plan looks like it can be successful. Here is the opportunity to redefine the goals and expectations of the mentorship. Most mentorships fail because of unmet expectations or unrealistic goals. The redefinition stage allows for mid-course corrections as goals, expectations, and presuppositions meet reality.

During the redefinition stage, the mentor and mentoree should check to see if the key ingredients of a successful mentorship are present:

- Character (includes honesty in the relationship and the ability to positively respond to accountability questions)
- Clarity (clearly defined objectives)
- Communication
- Compatibility
- Consistency (in the performance of mentorship role and expectations)
- Compassion
- Correction (The mentor must be willing and able to provide correction when necessary, and the mentoree must be willing and able to receive it.)

Once any necessary redefinition of the mentorship occurs, implementation of the mentoring process can continue from this point.

DEPARTURE

The departure stage is one of the most important events in the mentorship. At this stage, the mentor and mentoree transition from a formal mentorship to a traditional peer relationship. This departure stage assumes that the mentorship has successfully run its predetermined course. However, it is at this stage that difficulty can occur since the mentor and mentoree will disengage from a somewhat concentrated relationship to one that is less structured with less frequent interactions.

It is important that it is clearly understood that as the mentorship comes to a conclusion and the nature of the relationship changes, there is no less of a commitment on the part of the mentor to the success of the mentoree for their personal life and ministry.

RECONNECTING

Reconnecting is the stage at which the mentor and mentoree actually reconnect in a new relationship. The new relationship is now that of peers and friends. If the departure stage goes well, then the reconnecting stage should go well. The mentor and mentoree should show intentionality in reestablishing their relationship. This may occur through social contacts, family outings, joint ministry endeavors, etc.

If a mentoring relationship is to be successful, both mentor and mentoree are strongly encouraged to make three commitments from the outset:

- *To the Lord*—that each may fulfill this mentorship in order to better serve Him.
- *To one another*—that each may seek to establish a strong and caring relationship and make the most of this opportunity.
- *To the actual requirements of the mentoring program*—that each will fulfill every component of the program in order to maximize the effectiveness of this mentoring relationship in the life of both the mentor and mentoree.

Each of us must ask ourselves two questions: Who am I and what am I doing with my life? We have each been called and chosen to accomplish certain things. We can learn from the past, but we must live in the future. Mentoring, as modeled by Jesus, can be an excellent tool for the development of our life for service to God and the church. Ultimately, we must spend time each day with our heavenly Mentor so that we can be formed and qualified by Him.

Ronald Maddox completed his B.A. degree at Southeastern College of the Assemblies of God, Lakeland, Florida. He has done graduate studies at Florida State University. He completed his M.A. and M.Div. programs at Assemblies of God Theological Seminary, Springfield, Missouri, and is currently in a doctoral program there. Maddux has served with Assemblies of God Foreign Missions since 1977, in both Hong Kong and Thailand. He served as an area director in Asia Pacific for ten years and is currently the regional director for Northern Asia. Maddux is married and has three children.

17

Battered Yet Standing

DAVID L. STEVENS

"This is not what I expected. When I gave my life to Jesus, I thought things would be much easier. Yet here I face greater problems and more of them than before. What am I doing or not doing that has caused all of this to come my way?"

Sound familiar? Sure, we often hear the testimony of someone who, having accepted Jesus as Savior, tells of all the problems that seemed to vanish and the many unexpected blessings flowing their way.

It is true that the Lord has given us the greatest gift of all, the gift of salvation. It is also true that many who love the Lord and are committed to Him find themselves facing adversity.

Jesus tells a story of such man in Matthew 7:24-27. While this man was trusting fully in Christ, he was still subjected to a great storm. In fact, it was the same storm that came upon the foolish man who built his house upon the sand. Jesus paints a vivid word picture with this story. He compares the man whose house was built upon the rock to one who hears, believes, and receives Him and is committed to flowing His Word. The foolish builder upon the sand is different. Jesus compares him to those who hear Him but reject Him and put their trust in someone or something else.

Notice how the storm affects the two. While the storm has battered and beaten both houses, only one remains standing. The storm indeed batters both houses. The one on the rock, though made with superior wisdom and craftsmanship, did not escape the storm's fury.

"And the rain descended, and the floods came, and the winds blew, and beat upon that house; and if fell not: for it was founded upon a rock" (Matthew 7:25, KJV).

Jesus never promised problem-free living. He promised there would be times of hardship and adversity, regardless of one's position or assets.

Jesus himself experienced times of weariness, weeping, and hurt. He faced opposition and endured adversity. There are those who would say that because Jesus faced all of that, His followers don't need to. Yet Jesus made it clear we also would face great adversity, even with a deep commitment to follow Him. This certainly does not sound like a good selling point if one is trying to get someone to follow Christ. But we are not in the sales business. We are in the business of life—dealing with real issues that people face—and we must always be truthful about what people can expect when they choose to follow Christ.

STORMS WILL COME

When John the Baptist baptized Jesus, God spoke from heaven saying, "This is my beloved Son, in whom I am well pleased" (Matthew 3:17). In the next verse (4:1), the Holy

Spirit led Jesus into the wilderness to be tempted of the devil. Jesus was not surprised that the devil showed up; He expected it and was prepared for him.

Even when you are approved by God and are led by the Holy Spirit, you are going to encounter adversity. Yes, many problems that people deal with are indeed of their own making. Perhaps disobedience, neglect, or carelessness in heeding God's Word have caused them to reap what they have sown. But one can be in God's will, led by the Holy Spirit, and still face adversity.

A brother in the church in which I grew up would make it a point to meet new converts, usually before they could get off their knees at the altar. He would tell them that they should get ready for an all-out attack of the devil now that they had decided to follow Jesus. Some might not agree with such an approach. Some may think it's too negative or too likely to dampen the joy of a new convert. But I never witnessed a loss of joy in any of those new believers. In fact, they seemed to appreciate it, especially when he would add that no matter what comes, the Lord would bring them through it.

Many Christians, when faced with a storm, feel they must have missed something or that the Lord isn't pleased with them. They become discouraged and confused.

Jesus said, "In the world ye shall have tribulation" (John 16:33, KJV). He wasn't speaking to unbelievers but to His own. But let me hasten to give you the rest of that verse: "But be of good cheer; I have overcome the world." You are going to face adversity. Nevertheless, you are going to make it because you are in Christ Jesus and He has already overcome. It's a done deal.

YOUR HOUSE WILL STAND

Jesus said the reason the house remained standing was its foundation. The rock made the difference. He said nothing about the house's décor, style, or size. It was all about the foundation, the rock.

Churches vary in size, structure, and style. Yet when a storm comes, the thing that matters most is the foundation. A firm one will hold everything together. The apostle Paul writes, "For other foundation can no man lay than that is laid, which is Jesus Christ" (1 Corinthians 3:11). Jesus is the only sure foundation; all others stand on sinking sand. So what if the stock market takes a dive or even if all we have accumulated is somehow lost? It will hurt. But this is not our security; we have built our hope on Jesus and He never fails.

Jesus describes the power of the storm, but there is no statement that either of these builders deserved to be battered by it. Isn't it amazing how many have an opinion about why some faithful follower of Christ is suddenly facing adversity? Some will claim it is the devil at work. Others believe it is God testing them—and their faith is not strong enough. Still others recognize, "It's just life; it rains on the just and unjust. Adversity is a part of life." No matter why one thinks the adversity has come, it must be dealt with.

PERSONAL STORMS

It has been more than two years since I returned from a missions tour through Europe. I kept an appointment for a simple routine checkup. I was in good health and had no symptoms of any concern. The doctor, in the course of examination, found reason for concern. He found an area in my colon that looked suspicious, so he took a biopsy. A couple of days later, I was in my office at the church when his call came. He said, "Reverend, I'm sorry to inform you that my suspicions have been confirmed and you have a malignant cancer of the colon. We need to get you into surgery as soon as possible."

I had sat at that very desk for so many years listening to the stories of others who had faced such things and privately wondered how I might react to such news. As I thanked the doctor for his call and hung up the phone, I realized I was not moved. My joy and peace were in place, and at that moment the Holy Spirit brought to my mind a Scripture of assurance. It may seem strange, but that assurance was not that I would be healed even though I certainly do not doubt that the Lord is our healer. Nor was it assurance that the surgery would be successful although I had confidence it would be. My assurance was the same assurance Job had when he said, "He knoweth the way that I take" (Job 23:10). It was an assurance that the Lord was well aware I would face this; He had not been surprised. It was assurance that He already had a plan to bring me through. He would not fail me. My statement to God that day was not "Why?" but "Wow! How wonderful to know that You, God, have everything under control."

When adversity comes, it is natural to focus on the present difficulties. Yet Hebrews 12:2 says, "Looking unto Jesus the author and finisher of our faith; who for the joy that was set before him endured the cross, despising the shame, and is set down at the right hand of the throne of God."

The victory did not surprise Jesus. He faced the cross and all its shame and suffering, but His focus was beyond the cross, on the outcome. That is the answer for your life. It is following the example of Jesus, looking beyond the adversity to what you know God has promised as the outcome.

Some Scriptures are so familiar that people can quote them, but they fail to be in awe of such a promise. The Lord has given every believer this promise: "And we know that all things work together for good to them that love God, to them who are the called according to his purpose" (Romans 8:28). Jesus gives us the needed assurance. The house built on the rock took an awful beating, but the outcome was certain: It did not fall.

You may be up against something you've never been up against before. You may be dealing with feelings you have not dealt with before. Perhaps you feel like Jacob did when he found himself in a strange place and in a desperate situation. Jacob never imagined that in such a desolate locale he would have an encounter with God. But as Jacob lay on the ground with his head upon a stone, God gave him a promise that would change his life. Jacob was amazed when he said, "Surely the Lord is in this place; and I knew it not" (Genesis 28:16). So he called the place Bethel—"house of God."

When the storms of life come, never forget that no matter how hard the wind blows and beats against your life, the outcome is settled. The Lord is working everything together for good. The very place where you are right now—whether in sunshine or storm—is your Bethel. He is there.

YOUR STOM WILL END

Every storm has an end. The storm that beat against the house on the rock also came to an end. When Jesus was preparing His disciples for what He knew would be a time of great sorrow for them, He told them that in a little while they would not see Him, but then a little while later, they would (John 16:19). Jesus said they would indeed have sorrow but their sorrow would be turned to joy (v. 20). Just as He said, when He died at Calvary, their hearts were broken. But on Easter morning their sorrow turned to joy.

Your storm will end also. You cannot always escape adversity or the fury of the storm, but you will not be beaten down by it. Cling to God's promises. When the storm passes, you will stand victorious upon the Rock of Ages, Jesus Christ.

David L. Stevens is senior pastor of Eastside Assembly of God, Tucson, Arizona. Eastside Assembly is among the leading 100 churches in the Assemblies of God in missions giving. Stevens also is assistant superintendent and director of foreign missions for the Arizona District of the Assemblies of God and a general presbyter for the General Council of the Assemblies of God. He is on the advisory board for Media Ministries and International Media Ministries and is a board member for Western Bible Institute. He is a veteran of the Vietnam War, having served as a United States marine. Stevens and his wife, Hazel, have a son, Scott, who is married to Megan. They have one granddaughter, Hailey Renee.

18

Believing God's Word

DON BLANSIT

"Lord, make me like You; please make me like You." Christians have spoken this often in prayer or in song. This is frequently followed by, "Lord, let me become all that You want me to be—whatever it costs."

Little did I know what that meant until an early morning phone call on Tuesday, June 22, 1999. That call from my son, Chad, embarked my family on a journey that would challenge our faith and lead us to becoming more like Jesus.

"Karri is being rushed to the hospital," he said, "and we don't know what's wrong."

My daughter-in-law, who had given birth to our first grandchild six days earlier, had suffered a massive brain hemorrhage. Doctors gave her no hope of survival. At first they told us that surgery would be fruitless; but several hours later, it became necessary. A blood clot had formed, and there was no alternative but surgery. The procedure was risky, but Karri made it through. The doctors still offered no hope.

Two days later, I reluctantly left the hospital and went home to change clothes. Soon the phone range. The voice said, "Get back to the hospital; more bad news." I rushed back, immediately making my way to the intensive care unit. When I arrived, no doctor or nurse was in the unit. There had always been a nurse within arm's reach. Later I earned why they did not closely monitor Karri for several house. One of the hospital chaplains had told a pastor friend, "They have lost her. They are just allowing the family to pay their last respects."

I watched and prayed as my 24-year-old son—a young man upon whom god had placed a call to ministry—began to speak prophetically over his wife. The brain-pressure monitor had been in the high-60s range when I arrived. But as Chad began to speak life into his wife, he spoke to that monitor and said, "I command you in the name of Jesus to come down into the mid-20s range." My eyes were riveted to the monitor as I watched the machine drop into the upper 50s, then to the mid-50s, and down into the 40s. It continued dropping until it came to rest in the range of 20-25. I stood before my daughter-in-law and watched her come back to life.

Suddenly, a nurse came running into the room. She shined a flashlight into Karri's eyes; they looked normal. The nurse began to cry.

Chad asked, "You're seeing a miracle, aren't you?"

With tears streaming down her face, she whispered, "Yes."

Later she told the family, "I have worked in the neuro-trauma intensive care unit for four years and have never seen a miracle. But I have now."

God had brought Karri back from the brink of death.

On the following Tuesday my wife, Marquita, and I left the hospital for lunch. My cell phone range. Karri's brain was continuing to swell, and the doctors were recommending removal of a portion of her skull.

When we arrived back at the hospital, we were told Chad had gone to the church to pray. We started for the church immediately. As we were en route, God spoke to me: "You are going to sympathize with your son. He doesn't need your sympathy; he needs your strength." I determined that I was not going to leave the church until an answer came. God had been dealing with my son the same way. For three days we lived in the church, going home only to shower and change clothes.

Finally the doctor said, "It looks like she is going to survive."

Pastors grow accomplished at telling their people who are facing trouble, "It is going to be OK. God is in control." But what about when the problem is staring *you* in the face? At this writing, we have lived in this drama for nearly two years. Our faith has surged and it has grown weak, but we have stood on the Word.

DON'T GIVE UP

"Lord, make me like You," we pray. But we think, *Let it be easy. I will do anything for You as long as the cost isn't great.*

The greatest battle I have faced has been the guilt of being a faith preacher yet seemingly finding no answer to my own prayers. I was teaching an eight-week series on faith when this sickness hit my daughter-in-law. (That will make you examine your theology.) But if you are struggling with a similar doubt, let me encourage you. Don't give up. Though the circumstances may look bad—even impossible—the truth remains: There is nothing our God cannot do. After seeking God these many months, I am more convinced than ever of God's healing power.

After 17 months of doubt, fear, and questions, we found ourselves at our lowest point—on a weekend in November 2000. I had asked God, "Why are You being so cruel to my son? God, he has submitted to preach Your gospel, yet he can't fulfill his calling because he and his mother-in-law have determined to stay by Karri's side until the miracle comes." On that Saturday in November as I cried out to God in desperation, I discovered that my time of prayer was nothing more than a session of complaining, grumbling, and accusing God. Suddenly, I felt the Lord's presence, and He began ministering to me in a way I had never experienced.

He said, "Son, I love you, and I love your son. I love your son too much to be cruel to him. But I have had to bring him and you to the bottom so I could take everything out and remake you both according to what I desire."

But God wasn't finished. He said, "Chad can be like his father, sort of stubborn and bullheaded, so I have had to break him to make him a vessel of honor."

I never knew God spoke in that manner, but He pulled no punches that day.

BROKEN, LIKE JESUS

We tell God we want intimacy with Him, but we do not want to pay the price to live like Jesus. When I preached a message recently, "That I May Know Him—in Intimacy," God allowed me to see that intimacy comes through a broken spirit. Why is brokenness required? It is hard for carnal beings to surrender their wills. In most cases, before we are willing to surrender, we need to be broken. But as we realize we are unable to solve our problems, we learn total dependency upon God. At that point we can meet with Him openly and honestly.

That Saturday morning, November 11, 2000, there was no place to turn—and no one from whom to seek advice. It was God or else. I was a totally broken man—a man with many questions but no answers. In my brokenness God began to minister. Jesus demonstrated that to be like Him, we must be broken—broken by complete submission or by pain.

STANDING ON THE WORD

On that first Saturday after the illness came upon Karri,

the doctor had told the family that she had no more than 24 hours to live. With heavy hearts my son and I had gone to church the next morning to have the congregation pray for us. When Chad walked down the aisle of the church, they stood and gave him a standing ovation. It was an incredibly emotional moment. The church surged around us and began to pray. To this day our church stands strongly in the belief that Karri is going to be totally healed; they have been a tremendous source of strength.

All week long I had been mouthing the words, "She's going to be OK," but deep inside I had given up. As we were standing around the front with our people giving us so much love, God spoke into my spirit, "She's going to walk out of that hospital." I thought this would take place quickly, but Karri is still unable to care for herself or her baby.

In November 2000, God showed me that I had made something bad out of that prophetic word of Sunday, June 27. How? I had begun to place more confidence in that prophetic word than in the written Word of God. I had thought I had to somehow make it happen. God reminded me of the times I had preached, "No personal word of prophecy should ever take precedence over the written Word of God." But now I had allowed that to happen. God's mercy saw me through that.

Jesus, when tempted after 40 days of fasting, did not use man's wisdom nor did He seek out a spiritual person to give Him a personal word from heaven. Instead, he said to Satan, "It is written." If the Bible says it, stand upon that authority and claim your victory like Jesus did.

At this writing, our trial persists, and we continue to learn to rely on Jesus in the valley of testing.

If you want to be like Jesus, you must learn to follow

His example. Start now by standing in the face of great difficulties upon the authority of His Word. And remember to keep your eyes on Jesus, not on the circumstances.

Don Blansit graduated from Southwest Missouri State University, Springfield, Missouri, with a business degree in 1972. In 1973, God called him into ministry. In 1993, Blansit became senior pastor of Nixa Assembly of God, Nixa, Missouri. The church has an attendance of approximately 1,000 on Sunday mornings. Blansit and his wife, Marquita, have a son, Chad, and a daughter, RaChelle.

19

Faith-Filled Living

RICHARD A. PLUNK

The meeting had been called to discuss a new care group for our more mature church members. The current Empty Nesters had become too large. When I asked the leader if the group had thought of a name, he immediately said that he and his wife had been praying about Mountain Movers.

"Do you really think you can move mountains?" I teased.

"I don't see why not. The Bible says we can."

What a joy it was to hear this response from this seasoned, godly saint. I wonder if I would have received the same response from others.

In a day when many are running from any teaching on faith that really expects God to respond, it was exciting to see faith fleshed out in the heart and voice of one of my flock. Why shouldn't the Christian today ask and expect to receive from God? Why can't the believer expect God to move mountains at their request? Why can't we pray and believe that Jesus will heal? It is as if no one wants to believe God for the miraculous because we might be labeled an extremist. I am glad we have some faith folks in our congregation.

THE IMPORTANCE OF FAITH

The term *faith* seems to have taken on a life of its own in our society and in the church. It can be seen as good or not so good at all. We hear slogans like "blind faith," "leap of faith," and "keep the faith." There are whole schools on faith and new ministries emerging regularly that emphasize faith. But to become all that God wants us to become, it *will* take faith being put into action.

Why is faith so important? Throughout the life of Jesus, when He saw faith, He appreciated the individual who demonstrated it — such as the centurion in whom Jesus saw great faith (Matthew 8:10).

Jesus did not hesitate to rebuke when faith was limited or lacking as with the disciples during the storm in Mark 4:40. Jesus called for disciples to simply "Have faith in God" (Mark 11:22, NIV).

Paul taught the importance of faith in the life of the believer. The just live by faith (Romans 1:17); we walk by faith and not by sight (2 Corinthians 5:7). Ultimately, without faith it is impossible to please God (Hebrews 11:6).

In his book, *Fresh Faith,* Jim Cymbala emphasizes the importance of faith: "Nothing else counts if faith is missing. There is no other foundation for Christian living, no matter the amount of self-effort or energy spent. Nothing else touches the Father's heart as much as when His children simply trust Him wholeheartedly."[1]

Hebrews defines faith as "the substance of things hoped for, the evidence of things not seen" (11:1, KJV). Moffat includes the words "confident" and "convinced" in his definition. Faith is simply taking God at His word. Faith is being convinced that God's Word works even when we don't see the evidence before us.

Where do I get this faith? It is from God. Romans 12:3 indicates that God has given each individual a "measure of faith." You have some already. Without faith, you cannot become a Christian. We are saved by grace through faith (Ephesians 2:8). So we must have faith to appropriate God's grace which is the beginning point of salvation. This faith must be built up and added to. Paul tells us faith is built by hearing the Word of God (Romans 10:17). We don't pray for it, beg for it, or plead for it. It grows within us as we spend time in God's Word and discover more about Him. We cannot have real faith in God apart from His Word. The more time we spend in God's Word the more we are convinced of its relevance for today.

ACTIVATING FAITH

What can you receive by using faith? We have already seen that your salvation comes from God's grace through your faith in Him to save you. Jesus responds to a young woman in the house of Simon the Pharisee, "Your faith has saved you" (Luke 7:50, NKJV). She was told to go in peace. Not only did her faith bring her forgiveness of her sins but also the blessing of Jesus to go on her way in the peace that comes from that forgiveness. So from faith, she received peace and forgiveness.

Jesus met two blind men. "According to your faith let it be to you," He said (Matthew 9:29). Their sight was restored immediately. Faith in the power of Jesus to heal brought the healing they needed. Jesus teaches that everything is possible for those who believe (Mark 9:23). James reminds us if we ask God for wisdom, believing in our hearts and not doubting, the Lord will give it to us (1:5-6), and that the prayer of faith will save the sick (5:15).

How do we release or activate our faith? How can I put it into action so I can enjoy the same benefits received by people who had faith in Jesus' day? Do what they did: Use it. Jesus asks us to step out in faith and trust Him. Peter would never have walked on the water had he not responded to Jesus' invitation to come to Him. The woman with the issue of blood received her healing by believing that by merely touching Jesus, she could have her healing. We must trust God and His Word. Just do it; believe it.

Releasing and using our faith in God assumes an understanding that we ask and receive only those things that are in agreement with His Word. The Word of God will reveal His will and His character in regard to our lives. The more we know about the will of God and the character of God, the more we understand how He will respond to us. If we know that we are praying in God's will, we know that He hears us. And if we know He hears us, then we have the petitions we ask of Him (1 John 5:15). That builds our faith in His response to our requests.

If faith is built by hearing the Word of God and spending time in God's Word helps us know more about the will and the character of God, it seems logical that our requests are then made from a position of greater faith.

Thus greater results are seen from our built-up faith, voiced from a greater knowledge of God.

ULTIMATE FAITH-BUILDER

The ultimate builder of our faith must be the ultimate revelation of God, Jesus Christ. Jesus is the Word of God who was made flesh among men. The character and will of God are revealed in the ministry of Jesus—in healing, forgiving, delivering, providing, working miracles, even in being raised from the dead. This was the ministry of Jesus. He did great things not simply because He was the Son of

God but also because He was anointed at His baptism with the Holy Spirit. This is the same Holy Spirit that is available to the believer today for anointed ministry.

The scriptural portrayal of Jesus in ministry also reveals the character of God with regard to His children. God is loving, merciful, compassionate, and full of grace to His beloved. In Christ we not only see these attributes of God but also understand the heart of Father God toward us when we pray and ask in faith for our needs.

My daughter, because she knows my love for her, is likely to ask me for something she needs or something special she desires. She knows my heart by spending time with me, hearing my words, and watching me touch the lives of others. God longs for His children to discover His desire to give good gifts to those who are part of His family. This knowledge makes us more willing and eager to seek Him for the things we need and desire.

What can bring our faith down? Jesus rebukes His disciples in Luke 12 for having little faith. They were worrying about what they would wear and eat. He draws attention to the lilies of the filed: They don't even work yet they were more splendid than Solomon in all his finery. Worry was a great defeater of faith—even in those who accompanied Jesus and saw victorious faith in action.

Worry can be a great crippler of disciples today who fail to trust in God. When the disciples worried about feeding the 5,000, Jesus took over with a miracle of provision from a small boy's lunch.

The provision of Jesus comes from His power, not from what we have to offer. But His power is put into motion by our faith, knowing God's will and character.

It is not only worry that lessens faith; fear can have the same effect. Jesus asked His disciples in the little boat why they were so afraid. He stilled the storm by a miracle of the Spirit of God. The miracles available to Christ in His day are available under the same anointing of the Spirit on the body of Christ today. Fear can be like a chokehold on the believer, causing them to give way to doubt. Fear should be replaced by faith in a never-changing God.

"Don't worry; be happy" were the words to a popular song. That is a sentiment I greatly appreciate. Sometimes it seems as if every phone call and visitor to the office brings more reports of bad things happening to God's people and our church family. When believers go through times like these, it is easy to let worry, doubt, and fear ease in the door. The more we let it, the more life can cause our attitudes to get us down. We have to take control; we must change our outlook and our confession.

Your attitude can make a significant difference in living the victorious life of faith in Christ. Some folks would be more victorious in life if they just smiled...once.

Jesus says that you speak out of the abundance of your heart. If your life is filled with faith in God, your mouth should speak such fullness. Life is overflowing with folks who will talk you into gloom and doom so that your own words become negative. Don't let them have that influence. Let your heart's fullness of faith flow out from you to touch others. Perhaps a better lyric than those of the aforementioned song would be, "Don't worry; be believing." For believing in God will bring happiness.

Faith is foundational to the Christian being able to live a victorious life. Though books on self-help and tapes on self-improvement are readily available, our best avenue is to fill our hearts with the Word of God. That is how we build our faith and activate the power of Almighty God on our behalf. Remember, Jesus was the ultimate man of faith; and without faith, it is impossible to please God.

Richard A. Plunk, D.Min., has served as senior pastor of Grace Community Assembly of God in Flower Mound, Texas, since 1995. He holds the D. Min. from Fuller Theological Seminary, Pasadena, California; M. Div. from Southwestern Baptist Theological Seminary; and a B.A. in biblical studies from Evangel University, Springfield, Missouri. He previously pastored Lighthouse Assembly of God, For Worth, Texas, and served as associate pastor at Southside Assembly of God in Garland, Texas. He served in the North Texas District of the Assemblies of God from 1990-97. Plunk and his wife, Ladonna, have two children: Todd and Haley.

20

The Christian and Community Impact

JOHN P. KUERT

To most Christians, making a spiritual impact on a community typically means organizing a big event. They assume the need for some type of evangelistic crusade, concert, or witnessing invasion. This, of course, requires extensive planning and organization as well as lots of time and money in order to see great numbers of people swept into the kingdom.

There is certainly a place for mega-events to reach the masses—especially if they help Christ's followers develop a burden for the lost. But this is not the primary model Christ gave us. When Jesus called His disciples, He set a model of ministry that started with touching the lives of individuals who would, in turn, influence others. If each member of the body of Christ would adapt Jesus' strategy and focus on the difference the individual can make, our communities would be impacted far more rapidly and effectively than if we continue our dependency on event evangelism as the primary means of reaping the harvest.

Several years ago my family and I were visiting Germany. One day, as I was following the Romantic Road through the countryside, I came to an unmarked intersection and realized I was lost. A local farmer tried his best to give me directions in German, but I wasn't getting it. As I saw his frustration level rising, I pretended to understand and politely thanked him. I turned right and started in the direction he pointed; but after a few miles and still no markers, I decided that the most sensible thing to do was to backtrack. My family protested. After all, what would the farmer think? Nevertheless, I headed back. When we approached the intersection, my wife and children slumped down in the car. I have always wondered what the farmer thought as he saw me waving and driving in the opposite direction without my family. But it was the right move because we were heading in the right direction.

It's time for us as believers to retrace our steps and get back to the kind of individual involvement that caused the Early Church to impact the first century.

Not only is this what Jesus originally intended, but it will also be the most effective way for us to reach our generation. Today we are faced with reaching secular people who have built up so many barriers of resistance to the institutional church and religion that it's going to take individuals building personal bridges.

Unfortunately though, most Christians never go beyond theoretical belief. We want to make a spiritual impact, but we're not sure how to get our lives going in that direction. We dream of influencing our community for Christ, but the sad reality remains that most have never even led one person to Christ. Whatever the reasons may be for this condition, it is imperative we overcome our inertness and start to make a difference.

To impact someone is to have an effect on them or influence their thinking. Here are some signposts that will help us to get to that destination, using the acronym IMPACT as a guide.

INFILTRATION

In John 17, as Jesus was about to complete His mission on earth, He prayed for His disciples to be in the world but not of the world. As far back as I can remember, our main emphasis on that prayer was a Christian lifestyle of holiness and separation from the world. While this was certainly a part of what Jesus had in mind, a more balanced view is to understand that He was praying for us to maintain our distinctiveness as His disciples while being in the world as His witnesses.

Unfortunately, our imbalanced emphasis against worldliness has produced a mentality that has caused us to withdraw from the world for fear of contamination by it.

Consequently, we have developed a kind of Christian subculture characterized by isolationism. This protective mentality has removed us from nonbelievers and has forced us into trying to make a difference from a distance.

In order to make a spiritual impact, the first step is to *infiltrate*. We must be out there where the people are. Jesus taught us that we are the light of the world, but what good is light if it only shines where there are other lights? It's time for Christians to come out of hiding and become more visible. The world at its darkest needs the church at its brightest. Of course, we must be careful not to compromise as we venture into the world, but we can no longer remain aloof.

MINISTRY MIND-SET

Ministry is a key New Testament word, but it is often misunderstood. While mostly used in a professional ecclesiastical sense today, the word for ministry in the New Testament, *diakonos,* means to serve others. People and churches that are making the greatest impact on their communities have discovered the potential of serving and ministering to others—even in seemingly menial ways—as a first step in bringing people toward Christ.

When Jesus came into the world, He stated His objective: "I came to seek and to save what was lost." His first step, however, in closing the gap between God and humanity was to compassionately reach out to people and help them where they were. From the outset of His ministry, He went about doing good and demonstrating the unconditional love of God. Jesus knew that before He could get their hearts, He had to get their attention. By ministering to people and meeting them at their point of need, Jesus began to tear down people's defenses and build an attitude of openness so they would receive the good news of the kingdom.

In today's world where people have built up so many walls of resistance to the church, one of the best ways to break through those barriers is to apply this same approach Jesus used. As we infiltrate our world, we need to go with a *ministry mind-set* that is looking for ways to show the unconditional love of Christ through caring, helping, and doing good. By beginning at the level of people's felt needs and aspirations, we start to bridge the distance from indifference to faith.

PARADIGM SHIFTS

In the past, our approach to evangelism has been church-centered; our approach to ministry, pastor-centered;

our approach to discipleship, do-it-yourself centered. In other words, ministry has been the responsibility of the pastor, winning people to Christ had to take place within the walls of the church and discipleship was a process that we assumed each individual convert would undertake on their own. Most of us have lived within the framework of these familiar patterns in the church. This has consequently greatly undermined individual responsibility.

If we hope to have a greater impact in the 21st century, we must realize that each believer is called to be an active participant in all three of these areas. We must realize that the work of the ministry is to be shared by everyone. We need to break out of the mold that has kept evangelism confined within the walls of the church building. We must revive Jesus' mobilization mentality which focuses on taking the good news to where people are. We have to place a greater emphasis on the responsibility of each Christian to personally disciple and mentor new believers to maturity.

AUTHENTICITY

This is a real dilemma for true believers because one of the qualities that the new generation values most is authenticity.

Even though we are living in days of unprecedented hunger for spiritual truth and experience, the world is not looking to the church for answers. Instead, people are looking to various religious alternatives. A big part of the problem is the church's image in the eyes of secular society. Between the media's spin which usually portrays Christianity in a bad light and the faddish hype that we have produced from within our ranks, people have concluded that the church is overrun with hypocrisy.

We must ask, "How can we change our image in a skeptical environment where all Christians are lumped together and caricatured as a bunch of phonies?"

To overcome this stereotype, we can start by building relationships with people so they can get to know us up close and see that we are genuine. The greatest public relations campaign a church can muster cannot compare with the solid impact an individual believer can have by letting the world see that Christians are authentic. Once people see what we are, they are much more open to what we have to say. If we would only take the time to bridge this gap of authenticity, we would undoubtedly be more influential. People today have been given much more exposure to what is out of the mainstream of orthodox Christianity than to what is genuine. The best way for us to bring people closer to a decision for Christ is to stop doing witnessing and start being His witnesses.

COMPASSION

Compassion must underlie all our efforts to reach people. We can change methods, shift paradigms, get an image makeover, repackage the message, and reinvent the church; but without the compassion of Christ, our methods are reduced to marketing strategies.

To make a difference, we must, like Jesus, have a heart of true compassion.

When Jesus saw the multitudes, He was moved with compassion. This is the first aspect of true compassion that is characterized by an inner emotional response that empathizes with people. When it comes to compassion, this is where most of us stop—with a feeling. Jesus went beyond this. He didn't just identify with people; His heart of compassion motivated Him to action. That's the kind of compassion we need to have—compassion that compels us to make a difference. We can have great aspirations to influence our world; but until we take action, nothing will happen. Someone has said that the smallest obedient act is better than the greatest intention.

TRUTH THAT'S RELEVANT

We must also learn to take the first-century message and put it in a 21st-century package. We must pay attention to the apostle Paul's words: "I have become all things to all men so that by all possible means I might save some" (1 Corinthians 9:22, NIV). He showed a tremendous understanding of the need for relevance which is often missing in the church today. Instead of finding new and creative ways of communicating the old, old story, we expect the world to adapt to our style, our language, our methods. The question we have to wrestle with is, "Who adapts to whom?" Just as missionaries must relate to the culture in which they minister, so we all must find ways and means to bring the gospel to our communities in ways they can understand. Isn't this exactly what Jesus did for us by bringing heavenly truth in earthly terms?

As we face the new challenges of the 21st century, let's remember the saying, "God and I make a majority." If we really believe that, then the words *impact* and *individual* definitely go together.

Go make a difference in your world.

John P. Kuert has spent most of his 33 years of ministry in the greater Pittsburgh area. Since 1980, he has been senior pastor of Evangel Heights Assembly of God, Sarver, Pennsylvania. He has led the church in this rural suburb to become a vibrant congregation. They have developed a strong witness in the surrounding communities and have also become a leading church in foreign missions giving, supporting more than 60 missionaries in 40 countries. In five phases the church has built a complex of 52,000 square feet and has established many ministries including a Christian academy and preschool and a Christian radio station. Kuert is a graduate of Valley Forge Christian College, Phoenixville, Pennsylvania, and Assemblies of God Theological Seminary. Kuert and his wife, Sandy, have been married for 32 years and have a daughter and son who are also involved in ministry.

21

Generosity: Gateway to Greatness

MARK J. ANTHONY

Narcissus, a character in ancient Greek mythology, was a young man in love...with himself. Sitting by a pool of water, he became captivated by his own reflection. Day after day he would gaze at himself. He was so absorbed with self-love that he lost all his friends. One day his feelings became so strong that he leaned over to kiss his own reflection and drowned.

Psychologists have named one of our culture's chief character flaws *narcissism*. Our culture is obsessed with self-achievement and never satisfied with present status. Most people are not interested in eternal salvation but crave external approval. Self-fulfillment is the ultimate goal.

Today even the church is infected with narcissism. The Lord's disciples must march to a different drumbeat: self-sacrifice and humility. Whereas the mantra of the world seems right and logical, the chorus of God's kingdom appears paradoxical. Jesus told His disciples, "If anyone desires to come after Me, let him deny himself, and take up his cross, and follow Me. For whoever desires to save his life will lose it, but whoever loses his life for My sake will fine it" (Matthew 16:24-25, NKJV).

Unfortunately, many have focused on upward mobility and self-gratification. On the one hand, one might say, "If I focus on personal achievement now, then I will be better equipped to help the unfortunate later." On the other hand, the follower of Christ might say, "I will walk daily in obedience to the Master's will and find joy and fulfillment in Him alone." The believer understands that charity has little to do with outside circumstances and much to do with the spiritual condition of the heart. Generosity is the gateway to greatness, and its measure is found in attitude, not in assets. Mother Teresa believed, "The more you have the less you can give, and the less you have the more you can give."[1] A recent study showed that poorer Americans give a greater percentage of their income to charity. In 1998, those who earned less than $10,000 averaged 5.2 percent given; those earning $10,000 to $19,000, 3.3 percent; those earning $75,000 to $99,999, 1.6 percent.[2]

Followers of Christ should be the most generous people in the world because they understand that wealth consists not in the abundance of possessions but in one's identity as a child of God.

Jesus still honors the generosity of the widow more than the substantial, unsacrificial gift of the affluent. Why? In God's economy, generosity is a matter of the heart.

A preacher asked a farmer, "If you had $200, would you give $100 to the Lord?"

"Sure would," said the farmer.

"If you had two cows, would you give one cow to the Lord?"

"Yeah, I would."

"If you had two pigs, would you give one of them to the Lord?"

The farmer replied, "That's not fair. You know I have two pigs."

Let's look at three principles of generosity from John 3:16.

DIVINE EXAMPLE: "FOR GOD SO LOVED THE WORLD"

When billionaire Howard Hughes died, naked and paranoid, someone asked how much he left. The answer: "All of it." The ultimate measure of a man's wealth is how much he is worth when he has lost everything.

Job understood the source of fulfillment as he worshipped God during a tumultuous time: "Naked I came from my mother's womb, and naked shall I return there. The Lord gave, and the Lord has taken away; blessed be the name of the Lord" (Job 1:21).

God owns everything. His very nature opposes selfishness. There has never been a greater gift in the history of mankind than the heavenly Father's gift of His own Son. God bankrupted heaven to purchase the salvation of man. Jesus would ultimately take the government of humanity upon His shoulders to produce order in the midst of chaos. But before His rule and reign, Jesus would shoulder the cross to bear the sins of the world in His body. The King of kings deserved the crown of glory but instead received a shameful diadem of thorns and gave His life willingly for a people who rejected Him. Generosity is a natural expression of the character and nature of God. "For God so loved the world that He gave His only begotten Son."

Paul said, "For you know the grace of our Lord Jesus Christ, that though He was rich, yet for your sakes He became poor, that you through His poverty might become rich" (2 Corinthians 8:9). Believers are more apt to lay down their nets of personal ambition if there is an honest evaluation of the sacrifice and model of heaven. When believers are able to follow Christ without the weight of greed, the end result is inevitably fulfillment. Generosity may not be a natural inclination, but the sacrifice of Calvary empowers disciples to overcome narcissism and become conduits of God's gracious gifts.

DIVINE EXPRESSION: "HE GAVE"

Love is the driving force of generosity. The verb "loved" in John 3:16 is the main focus of the verse. Jesus is letting us know that the love of the Father is what brought about the Incarnation. True love will always produce action. It is not some ethereal intention of a good-natured brother. The love of God is tangible. This idea is modeled by our heavenly Father but seen too little in church life.

In Luke 10:29, a lawyer asks who his neighbor is. T.W. Manson doesn't believe the question should even be asked, "for love does not begin by defining its objects; it discovers them."[3] Nevertheless, the lawyer asked.

Jesus tells a parable in reply, and it is clear that those figures most likely to help a needy person fail when the ultimate test arrives. An anonymous man (we'll call him Joe) is stripped, beaten, and left for dead along a dark, narrow country road. Because of the man's condition, no passerby would be able to tell what ethnicity or religious community he belongs to. He is just a wounded man. Who will provide assistance?

The local pastor would be the logical choice. He has just come from his church feeling pretty good because the sun was shining, the pews were full, and the offering plates were overflowing. Joe may be in luck. Professional ministers surely assist the unfortunate. But after seeing the need, the pastor delivers a short compassionate prayer while continuing to drive. One can't really fault the pastor; he couldn't even tell if Joe was a member of his church. He might have inconvenienced himself if he had at least been a member of his denomination, but he could not risk being late to an important committee meeting.

But Joe seems to be fortunate. A deacon is driving close behind his pastor. Deacons are always willing to serve the needy. The deacon steps out of his car to determine the severity of the injury. Unfortunately, the deacon cannot determine whether Joe is his neighbor because he is unrecognizable. The deacon kneels to offer a sincere prayer for the less fortunate and then steps back into his car and leaves Joe.

Nothing could prepare Joe for what happens next. An atheist drives to the curb and is moved with compassion. The pastor looked out his window, the deacon stepped out of the car, but the compassion of the atheist motivates him to nurse Joe back to health. He doesn't allow his schedule, his wallet, or any prejudicial concerns hinder the outreach to a man seen as an inconvenience by very religious people.

If Jesus would have told a story of a faithful church member helping an annoying atheist, it could have been easier to swallow, but to make the atheist the hero is appalling. This bold story is not going to win Jesus any popularity contests; then again, He is not running for office. He has an appointed position.

For Jesus, love and generosity are not a creed but a commitment that requires action. In essence, the Lord's answer to the lawyer's question is: "You must be a neighbor to anyone who has a need—including the one who lives on the other side of the religious, political, social, racial, or economic tracks."

Paul challenged the Corinthian church in the arena of generosity: "I am testing the sincerity of your love by the diligence of others" (2 Corinthians 8:8). The Lord is not impressed with religious rhetoric but smiles upon a Samaritan's thoughtful intervention.

DIVINE EXTENSION: "WHOEVER BELIEVES IN HIM"

God gave His only Son but has multiplied the family of God by releasing the greatest gift ever given. Our gifts persevere through the limitations of the present to unknown possibilities. It was evident that Albert Einstein was convinced of the necessity of personal investments into society when he said, "A hundred times a day I remind myself that my inner and outer life depends on the labors of other men, living and dead, and that I must exert myself in order to give in the measure as I have received and am still receiving."[4] The resources of this world are temporary but, when given away, are made eternal.

Generosity confirms our testimony to the world: "Because of the service by which you have proved yourselves, men will praise God for the obedience that accompanies your confession of the gospel of Christ, and for your generosity in sharing with them and with everyone else" (2 Corinthians 9:13, NIV).

Heather Hubble was an ordinary 14-year-old girl who had an extraordinary dream. In 1997, it looked like Russia was going to be closed to the gospel soon. Heather was so moved by the possibility of providing Bibles to Russian children that she told her local

Missionettes director that she wanted to personally raise $1,000. This was unrealistic in light of the fact that the entire district had given $7,487 the previous year. Still, while living with four siblings in a single-parent home, Heather believed in prayer, work, and personal sacrifice. Though there were times of discouragement, Heather said, "If you pray, stuff happens." By the end of the year she had given more than $1,000 to buy Bibles for children she would never meet. Only heaven knows who has been born into the kingdom of God as a result of the generosity of this 14-year-old girl.

A generous spirit is multiplied beyond the initial touch for it inspires other believers to live courageously and provokes the seeker to consider the goodness of God.

Many were inspired by Heather's faith. In 1998, the Missionettes of the Georgia District of the Assemblies of God gave almost $30,000; in 1999, more than $50,000. The Heather Club was formed for those who would give $100 or more to missions in a given year.

Does your life resemble the character and nature of Christ? Believers are challenged to rise above the effects of narcissism that so pervades this culture and human nature and to "love thy neighbor as thyself." The clarion call from the heavens is to resist the inclination to hoard and become a vessel of God's grace to a world that has been robbed, stripped naked, and left for dead.

Mark J. Anthony is a graduate of Christ for the Nations Bible Institute, Dallas, Texas; and Southeastern College of the Assemblies of God, Lakeland, Florida. He accepted Christ at the age of 5. He has ministered in more than 15 nations through music and preaching. Anthony is currently pastoring Trinity Fellowship Assembly of God in Sharpsburg, Georgia, and has been full-time pastoral ministry since 1992. He has a passion for equipping the saints to do the work of the ministry. Anthony and his wife, Julie, live in Newnan, Georgia, with their children, Caleb and Brooklyn.

22

Christians Must Be Violent

RUSSELL W. EGGERT

One word not frequently connected with Jesus is *violence.* Jesus is the Prince of Peace, the meek Miracle Worker, Timid Teacher, and Suffering Servant. He is the undeserving victim and the author of "turn the other cheek." Jesus was quick to say, "My time has not yet come" (John 2:4, NIV) at Cana. He rejects the use of violence at His arrest and heals Malchus's ear. Often His miracles are done outside the town, privately, or with the request to not make them pubic. He is depicted as the Lamb of God, not an aggressive, horned ram. As His ministry on earth nears its end, He appears to be the helpless, undeserving victim of political and religious intrigue out of control.

Throughout the Gospels, Jesus appears to avoid conflict. At Nazareth the crowd is about to throw Him off a cliff when He escapes. In Jerusalem He is challenged at His trial yet refuses to call His disciples or 10,000 angels to defend or rescue Him.

Then as Jesus is suspended between earth and sky, heaven and hell, we hear His cry, "It is finished" (John 19:30). Truth is revealed. He was in control all the time. At this moment of greatest crisis, earth and sky are torn and the veil of the temple is ripped from top to bottom. Through Scripture, we learn that death is defeated, the grave is robbed of its occupant, and the keys of hell are pulled from the hands of Satan. Violently Jesus demonstrates His power as the greatest enemies of man—sin, death, and hell—are defeated.

FORCEFUL LIVING

In Matthew 11:12, Jesus says the kingdom of God comes with violence and violent men take hold of it. The NIV rightly translates the word as "forcefully." The Greek word used here pictures someone forced to relinquish possession. Force is the component that propels the kingdom forward—a mighty power which even the gates of hell cannot withstand (Matthew 16:18).

The Bible is clear that there is opposition to the plan of God for man and earth. Since the fall of Satan and his banishment to the realm of earth, there has been a war between good and evil. One-third of the angels are fallen and oppose the will, rule, and plan of God.

There have been times in history during which the "inclination of the thoughts of [men's hearts] was only evil all the time" (Genesis 6:5). The Bible records that many individuals and nations have opposed God's purpose. Pharaoh is an example of a man who would not relinquish possession of the nation of Israel without being forced to do so. Even after the violence of the first nine plagues, Pharaoh hardened his heart; and it took the ultimate in force, the death of the firstborn, before God's people were released. Pharaoh's army comes to a violent end in the middle of the Red Sea.

From man's beginning in the garden and his ensuing ejection, it is obvious that the plan of God is not going to be accomplished without a fight. In the Old Testament, God is known as the God of battles (2 Chronicles 20:15; Psalm 24:8). Some object to the amount of violence in the Old Testament. We read of the flood, plagues of locusts and poisonous snakes, plagues of physical illness, and the earth opening up to swallow those who opposed divinely appointed leadership. The cities of Sodom and Gomorrah are destroyed by a rain of burning sulfur. Israel's enemies are conquered by hailstones, confusion (2 Kings 3; 2 Chronicles 20), blindness (1 Kings 16), and other nations that come to her rescue.

Some of the great heroes of Israel's past are men and women of war. The judges include men like Samson who killed many Philistines with the jawbone of an ass. Gideon, Barak, and Jephthah are listed among the heroes of faith (Hebrews 11:32). Even David, the king of the nation, was not allowed to build the temple because his hands were stained with blood.

The greatest kings of Israel and Judah as well as prophets are often seen casting down idols, smashing altars, and burning tools of idolatry. Not stopping there, they slay the prophets of false gods.

A SWORD

To understand this violence, we must first remember that it is not haphazard. The Bible is clear that God's force is directed at people intent on evil or people opposed to His plan and purpose. When sadly we find that the people of God themselves are the victims of the displeasure of God, it is because of their stubbornness and refusal to obey His law.

Is there a change in God between the Old and New Testaments? No. In Hebrews 13:8 and James 1:17, we are told that God does not change. The crucifixion of Jesus demonstrates that the opposition has not changed either; it is still strong.

Jesus clearly indicated that His coming was not intended to bring peace but a sword (Matthew 10:34)—a sword that will often divide a family and make the members within a household enemies. History reveals the frequent harsh and even violent reaction of family members to those converting to Christianity. *Foxe's Book of Martyrs* bears out the truth of Jesus' words. Throughout the A.D. era, believers have endured violence and severe persecution. Unfortunately, even the visible church has contributed at times with its own misguided violence, such as the Crusades, the Inquisition, internal feuds, witch hunts, and other sordid events that have stained her reputation.

It is important for us to understand that the enemies of God will not give up without a fight. When Jesus cast out evil spirits, He demonstrated that the strong man must be bound.

In Mark 9:14-32, the evil spirit came out violently. When Jesus was asked by His disciples why they were ineffective, His reply was, "This kind can come out only by prayer and fasting" (v. 29). The seven sons of Sceva in Acts remind us that we are in a spiritual battle for which we must be properly prepared.

The Christian life is not meant to be a life of ease. This is not an armchair religion. The repeated use of the words *discipline* and *disciple* should alert us to the rigor that is necessary. Many of the illustrations used in the New Testament refer to being a good soldier or athlete.

Coming to Jesus in a simple act of faith and asking for forgiveness allows you to become a true child of God. However, it also moves you from one side to the other. Although you may not have considered yourself a major player in the devil's camp, now you have become a member of God's army. In war the enemy doesn't ask what rank or job description you have. If you are wearing the uniform of the opposing side, you are the enemy.

Some people are shocked when they turn their lives over to God only to find that they are under fire. The apostle Paul only had a short time to stabilize his life in Christ before he found himself on the run. Let down through an opening in the wall of Damascus, he barely escaped with his life. That's just the beginning of an adventure that will see him stoned; beaten; imprisoned; shipwrecked; put in danger on all sides; and yes, even given a thorn in the flesh. In his day people were not always happy to hear the good news.

PREPARE FOR WAR

If we are going to live like Jesus in the 21st century, then we must prepare for spiritual war. The story of Job gives us great insight into the heartless tactics of Satan. He is prepared to destroy a "blameless and upright" man (Job 1:1). God allows Job's life to be ravaged so that all might see that his faith can withstand the loss of possessions, health, and even loved ones. In comparison, many Christians today whimper at the slightest inconvenience. Heaven help us if we come under heavy attack.

No one can say God's Word doesn't warn us. In fact, Paul in Ephesians 6 paints a clear picture of spiritual warfare.

We are not fighting against men and women but against spiritual power and forces of evil in heavenly realms. The devil does scheme to destroy our faith.

Thankfully, God has made every preparation for us to defend ourselves with spiritual armor and gives us an instrument with offensive power. The Bible, the sword of the Spirit, is sharp and two-edged. With this sword, we can cut the devil's lies apart and sever his grip on our lives.

During the Vietnam era, I was preparing to be a soldier of the cross, hoping to carry the message of peace anywhere my General would send me. Imagine my shock at getting my draft notice soon after graduating from Central Bible College. *God, there must be a mistake!* I prayed. Just a few months later, I was off to officer candidate school and then to pilots school.

Upon arriving at my base in Thailand, I found out quickly that the enemy we fought did not care that I was really a nice guy and a man of peace. Those bullets flying up at my plane sent a very clear message: This is war. Thankfully, God protected me *and* mentally prepared me for my subsequent ministry when the bullets changed to the fiery darts of a spiritual enemy.

War requires discipline. Situations demand immediate responses. When your commander says bank right, the surface-to-air missile hurtling at your plane gives no time for an explanation. When God speaks, we need to act. The Scripture is full of a sense of urgency. Time is short. The mission of our Commander is to rescue the perishing now.

We must recognize that the power given by the indwelling Holy Spirit is to help us do our part to propel the kingdom of God forward.

The Holy Spirit gives us a boldness to leave our comfort zone and step onto the battlefield in behalf of the lost and dying. Even the spiritual disciplines have a sense of violence in them.

We wrestle in prayer. Effective prayer requires energy and effort without regard for time, agenda, or physical discomfort. Fasting takes force: to subdue our passions and appetites is a real struggle. Tithing can even do violence to our checkbooks, but the long-term result is victory over possessiveness and a growing trust in God.

The Bible also describes the Christian life in athletic terms. We run a race. The race is not a short sprint but a marathon. We do not receive the prize until the end of the race. Paul's words to Timothy are: "I have fought the good fight, I have finished the race, I have kept the faith" (2 Timothy 4:7). We too are in a long-distance race.

God gave my family and me an opportunity to carry His message of peace to South Africa in the late 1980s. It was there that was introduced to marathon races. I learned quickly that you may be able to run a sprint without breaking into a sweat or experiencing pain, but a marathon is different. I have never experienced such a grueling test of physical stamina, mental pressure, and emotional drain. Each time as I neared 26 miles, every part of me hurt—even my hair. Reaching the finish line demands preparation, dedication, and discipline. It is no different in the spiritual race.

Living for Jesus—whether we think of it as a battle or a race—requires a use of force, buffeting our body into submission, resisting temptation, and defeating our spiritual enemy—just like Jesus did.

Don't be afraid. With God's help, pull down the strongholds of Satan, lay hold of the kingdom of heaven, and push back the gates of hell.

Russell W. Eggert, D.Min., is senior pastor of Marlton Assembly of God, Marlton, New Jersey. He holds master's degrees in biblical literature from Assemblies of God Theological Seminary, Springfield, Missouri, and in educational administration from Rowan University, Glassboro, New Jersey. He received a doctor of ministries degree from Trinity Evangelical Divinity School, Deerfield, Illinois. He has been in ministry for 30 years. He taught at Cape College of Theology

23

Lifestyle Evangelism

GEORGE H. SAWYER

Eric had worked hard. He had earned his MBA and gotten his first break with a large brokerage firm on Wall Street. Life was finally beginning to turn in his direction. Everything was almost as Eric had imagined. Almost. There was just this one thing—this empty place that would pull at the edges of his security. While he was busy at work or out with friends, he was rarely aware of its small voice; but when Eric would be alone and quiet, this unrecognized void would vie for his attention.

Generally, Eric would dismiss these thoughts. He never understood the origin of this inner tugging or its purpose; that is, until he met Matthew. Matt was intelligent, hard working, and certainly one of the up-and-comers of their firm. But there was more to Matt than the 9 to 5. If Eric had ever met anyone who seemed to have empty place in his life filled, it was Matthew. He was always consistent; he seemed to have a genuine inner peace.

Eric watched Matt and noticed his lifestyle was different from the other young executives. It had been a long time since Eric had read a Bible or attended church; but when he was around Matt, it seemed God wasn't far away. After a few weeks, Matt led Eric to Christ. Through Matt, Eric met the God who had been tugging at his heart. He discovered that Jesus could fill the void in his life as well. That's lifestyle evangelism.

Lifestyle evangelism is a foundational New Testament principle—a term used to describe the effects of committed Christians living out their faith in the midst of a searching society. Jesus declared, "You are the salt of the earth" and "You are the light of the world" (Matthew 5:13, 14, NIV). To fulfill Christ's purpose for His Church to impact society, we must remove the narrow concepts of modern-day evangelism and return it to the marketplace. We are in desperate need of liberation from current concepts that limit evangelism to a few within the body of Christ and select days on the calendar. We must understand that evangelism as a lifestyle is invasive, inviting, and inclusive.

INVASIVE EVANGELISM

The invasive quality of lifestyle evangelism deals with the ability and authority of the church to penetrate and invade society far beyond the four walls of our worship facilities. In Mathew 16, in the midst of Peter's great confession of Christ, we are also given Christ's great confession of the Church: "I will build my church, and the gates of hell will not overcome it" (v. 18). It is clear that the nature and position of the church is to be proactive and invasive.

We are to be salt and light. Salt is penetrating and preserving. It's greatest effect is realized not when bottled up but when spread around.

Jesus said of the light, "You are the light of the world. A city on a hill cannot be hidden. Neither do people light a lamp and put it under a bowl. Instead they put it on its stand, and it gives light to everyone in the house. In the same way, let your light shine before men, that they may see your good deeds and praise your Father in heaven" (Matthew 5:14-16). Light invades darkness. It overcomes it. Light is useless when hidden. It is wasted. The plan of Jesus Christ has always been for His people—His Church—to turn on the light wherever they live, work, and play by the way they live before watching men. That way unsaved people do not have to go to a building to meet Christ. Instead, every day, just like Matt with Eric, millions of Christians are taking the church to them. Countless points of light are invading the darkness, and men and women are seeing Christ.

When the church is triumphant, militant, and invasive, we have a greater understanding of Jesus' prayer in John 17. Jesus did not pray that the Father would take us out of the world but rather that He would protect us. Why not take us out of this conflict with evil? Because just as Jesus had been sent into the world, so He is sending us into the world. We are sent ones, so we can be seen ones. Paul says in 2 Corinthians 3:2, "Ye are our epistle written in our hearts, known and read of all men" (KJV). The great strategy of invasive lifestyle evangelism is that Christ is not restricted in waiting for lost people to come to Him; but through the lives of His followers, He is able to go to them.

INVITING EVANGELISM

Lifestyle evangelism also makes the good news inviting. One often most striking and unfortunate differences between the New Testament church and the version we have today is the loss of public respect and favor. The fall has been both precipitous and devastating. Even more alarming is the reality that most of the damage has been self-inflicted. The church is now too often characterized as weak and irrelevant at least and manipulative and dishonest at worst. As a friend of mine stated, "The world has done an incredible job of telling a lie, and the church has done a pitiful job of telling or living the truth." But this is not the final word on the subject.

There has never been a greater hour of opportunity for the church to impact this desperate generation. Think for a moment of the winsomeness of a life-giving church moving through a dying society.

We should be as attractive and inviting as streams flowing in the desert. Our greatest asset in evangelizing our world today is the lifestyle that only true believers are privileged to experience.

I read recently the testimony of the wife of one of the wealthiest and most powerful men in the world. This woman, who has all the creature comforts that can be imagined, was led to Christ by her chauffeur. How? Despite all she had, there was something in this man's life that she did not have—something inviting, something not for sale. Something already paid for by Christ that should so transform believers that it causes others to be curious. What a divine strategy. First Peter 3:15 tells us to "always be prepared to give an answer to everyone who asks you to give the reason for the hope that you have" (NIV). Because of Christ, our very lifestyle should cause the unsaved to desire the hope we possess. They should be asking us. Instead of waiting for the pastor to give an invitation, our lives become the invitation—right where we are, right where people's need is the greatest.

Let's examine the original model of this, the Early Church. "They devoted themselves to the apostles' teaching and to the fellowship, to the breaking of bread and to prayer. Everyone was filled with awe, and many wonders and miraculous signs were done by the apostles. All the believers were together and had everything in common. Selling their possessions and goods, they gave to anyone as he had need. Every day they continued to meet together in the temple courts. They broke bread in their homes and ate together with glad and sincere hearts, praising God and *enjoying the favor of all the people*. And the Lord added to their number daily those who were being saved" (Acts 2:42-47). What an exciting, Christ-honoring, inviting lifestyle. When believers love one another as we love Christ, all men will know that we are Christians. Can you imagine how effective our evangelism efforts would become if we "enjoyed the favor of all the people"? It was their loving, Christlike lifestyle lived out on a daily basis that gained them such favor. The unsaved Gentiles and the skeptical Jews of Jerusalem were impressed by the lives of these transformed men and women.

Without understanding the Christians' doctrine and even at the expense of their own tradition and culture, the populace of the city began to be attracted to and show favor toward these early believers.

And what was the result? "The Lord added to their number daily those who were being saved." The opportunity for people to come to Christ was never to be confined to certain days or buildings. Evangelism is intended to be the natural byproduct o Christians revealing Christ by the way they conduct their daily lives and relationships. "But thanks be to God, who always leads us in triumphal procession in Christ and through us spreads everywhere the fragrance of the knowledge of him" (2 Corinthians 2:14). The fragrance of God's presence draws searching men and women to Christ.

INCLUSIVE EVANGELISM

Lifestyle evangelism also has an inclusive quality. No one is left out. There are no reserves; no one is sitting on the bench. Everyone is on the front line in this battle for the eternal souls of men and women.

By God's design, every Christian's life becomes His message, His Word wrapped in human flesh.

The Church functions as the body of Christ. What we often fail to see is that body ministry is not only for the edification of the Church but also for evangelism. It seems we have safely hidden this lay ministry concept within the perimeters of our church buildings. It is vital that laity make the connection with their role in evangelism.

If every member of the body functions properly, then we have the opportunity to reveal Christ in His fullness. And what is the result? Scripture states that if Christ be lifted up, He will draw all men to himself. That's lifestyle evangelism. Members of the church are contact points for Christ in the lives of their friends, family, and fellow workers. Each member, in their own unique way, becomes an opportunity for those surrounding them to experience some measure of Christ. All of the varied personalities, talents, and abilities of the body of Christ weave their way through society and, under God's hand, a beautiful tapestry begins to emerge, revealing Christ. Every Christian, every member of the body, every thread of the tapestry are necessary if Christ is to be clearly seen by this searching generation.

These concepts of lifestyle evangelism are both relevant and effective for the 21st century. I have the joy of pastoring a vibrant, growing church that models this. For the last eight years, I have hosted a reception for our visitors following the Sunday morning worship service. I always ask the reason for their attendance that day. Almost 80 percent come by personal invitation. With all our promotion and advertising expertise, the fact remains that the vast majority of people come to church because of a personal invitation. Nothing can replace the effectiveness of a Christian's life on those who live and work around them.

Each year we have Easter and Christmas productions. This past Easter season we did nine performances with a combined attendance of 18,000. More than 65 percent of those who came indicated they attended due to a personal invitation. And this in a city of less than 60,000. We are able to be a congregation that represents every age level and every income level and has a racial and ethnic profile that matches our city demographics because of the effects of lifestyle evangelism.

When evangelism becomes a lifestyle that is invasive, inviting, and inclusive, the limitations are lifted from a local church and the possibilities of New Testament Christianity become a 21st-century reality.

George H. Sawyer is the founding pastor of Calvary Assembly of God in Decatur, Alabama, a growing multiethnic congregation with more than 100 ministries. Listed as one of Alabama's fastest-growing churches, Calvary was also named one of the top 300 Protestant churches in America by the Lilly Foundation Research Project 2000. Sawyer serves on the sectional presbytery and as a board member on several home and foreign missions ministries. He speaks at training and leadership conferences in the United States and abroad. He is the founder of the daily radio program Catch the Vision *and appears frequently on television as a host and guest. An honors graduate of Southwestern Assemblies of God University, Waxahachie, Texas, Sawyer was listed in* Who's Who Among Students in American Universities and Colleges. *He and his wife, Phyllis, have two daughters, Meredith and Nicole, and one granddaughter.*

24

Resurrection Living

EDDY BREWER

A teenager was struck by a car and seriously injured. His parents prayed for his recovery, as did everyone in the congregation they pastored. Nevertheless, doctors pronounced him dead.

His father continued praying in faith. God answered his prayer, and the young man was brought back to life.

That young man is my uncle, Ralph Hart, who has been preaching the gospel for more than five decades. For most of those years, he has pastored the same congregation in Detroit. He is a living tribute to the resurrection power of Jesus Christ.

The Gospels record not only the life and teachings of Jesus but also His death and resurrection. As Jesus was crucified and buried, the dreams of the disciples were shattered like a crystal vase dropped on a concrete floor. Despite His repeated predictions concerning His death and resurrection, the disciples were still not expecting Jesus to return to life after He was placed in the tomb.

Those who had been closest to Jesus gave up on their future plans—their roles in the kingdom they expected Jesus to establish. They should have been the most likely to retain hope that Jesus would return as He said He would. The situation looked hopeless. Sadness and disappointment enveloped them like a dark cloud covers the sky.

When the women went to the tomb that Sunday morning, they were not expecting what they found—a risen Christ. Their purpose was to see to a proper burial. Instead, they were greeted by angels who informed them that Jesus was alive. They hurriedly ran to share this news with the disciples, but the frightened men were reluctant to believe the reports that He was again alive.

When Jesus did reveal himself to His followers, He rebuked the 11 disciples for their lack of faith and their stubborn refusal to believe those who had seen Him after He had risen (Mark 16:14).

THE RESURRECTION CHANGES EVERYTHING

The Resurrection truly changed everything. It validated Jesus' claims. It confirmed His deity. It inspired confidence in His followers to preach the good news.

Although the words do not appear in Scripture, it is likely when the disciples discovered Jesus was alive that someone in the group must have said, "This changes everything!" If they didn't say it, they must have thought it.

The resurrection of Christ *did* change everything. His virgin birth was astounding. The miracles He performed were truly unexplainable in human terms. His teachings were beyond the limitations and mere understanding of average men. These were all evidences of His divine nature. But without the resurrection, Jesus would have merely been regarded as a good teacher or perhaps a prophet from God.

It gave them the determination and willingness to die for their faith.

Not only did the resurrection of Jesus change everything for the disciples, but it also changes everything for us today. Because of the resurrection, we can have life—abundant life now and eternal life for the future.

Jesus frequently used everyday stories with which His listeners could identify. To make things clearer to those to whom He was speaking, His teachings referred to things they would have been familiar with in their culture, such as agriculture and fishing. In John 10, Jesus gives a discourse on another common subject of His day—sheep. He states that true shepherds will always use the gate into the sheepfold. Anyone who attempts to enter another way, such as climbing over the side, is a thief and a robber.

In John 10:11, Jesus declares himself to be the Good Shepherd who lays down His life for the sheep. He says He is the door of the sheepfold (v. 9). Sandwiched between these two declarations is a verse in which Jesus gives His followers a strong warning, followed by a beautiful promise. "The thief comes only to steal, and kill, and destroy; I came that they might have life, and might have it abundantly" (John 10:10, NASV).

The warning is a reminder that Satan is constantly trying to destroy the lives of the sheep that are a part of God's flock. That is why the people of God need the protection of the true Shepherd.

But unlike the devil who comes to steal, kill, and destroy, Jesus promises His followers abundant life.

ABUNDANT LIFE

What does Jesus mean by abundant life? The New International Version translates it "life in all its fullness." By saying abundant life, does He mean our lives will be filled with riches and material possessions? Does He mean our schedules will be filled with activities?

The church I pastor is Abundant Life Assembly of God. The name was chosen from John 10:10. The community in which I live and the church I serve are fast-paced. The calendar is full of many events—good things, Christian things; but the sheer volume of them at times can be exhausting. When the calendar gets to be overwhelming, I have on occasion joked to my wife, "This abundant life is about to kill me!"

That is not what Jesus had in mind. The abundant life Christ refers to is not just having a full schedule with many things to do. He is not talking about having a bank account with more money than we need although He promises to provide for us. The abundant life is not just being blessed with many wonderful friends and a happy home.

The abundant life Jesus promises has more to do with spiritual blessings than physical and material ones. Spiritual blessings are those that cannot be purchased at the grocery store or ordered from a catalog.

The abundant life Christ promises consists of such things as a relationship with God through Jesus Christ. The abundant life He wants for us will contain peace—the peace of God that passes all understanding.

Joy is an evidence of the abundant life. In the midst of painful and even traumatic circumstances when Satan comes to steal our joy, Jesus promises to protect us if we will stay close to Him. Our joy can remain constant because of the abundance Christ provides for us.

The resurrection of Christ makes possible the abundant life He promised us. In Mark 5 Jesus brings a 12-year-old girl back to life. John 11 describes the raising of Lazarus from the dead. On several occasions Jesus brought to life those who were physically dead, but He spent more of His time bringing to life those who were spiritually dead. He does the same today. Because of His resurrection and because He did indeed conquer death, Jesus offers abundant life. Life that is genuine. Life that is full of meaning and purpose. Life that is eternal.

We can enjoy this abundant life now. Biblical examples remind us of the abundance Christ provides. With only five loaves and two fish, Jesus fed 5,000. After fishing all night with no results, Peter was asked by Jesus to take his boat out to deeper water and let down his nets. Peter obeyed, reluctantly. They caught such a large number of fish that their nets began to break. They called for help, and the catch was so great that both boats began to sink. That is abundant life.

CLOSE TO JESUS

Abundant life can only take place when Jesus is close by. It is totally dependent on having an intimate relationship with Him. And it is only possible because of the resurrection of Jesus. His resurrection truly changes everything.

In his book, *The Applause of Heaven*, Max Lucado tells the story of two men. In 1899, Dwight L. Moody, evangelist, and Robert Ingersoll, lawyer, orator, and political leader, died. Both were raised in Christian homes and spoke to large crowds, but their views of God differed.

Ingersoll was an agnostic; he made light of the Bible. Moody embraced the Bible as the hope for humanity and left behind institutions of education and churches. When Ingersoll died suddenly, people called his death tragic, and it came without the consolation of hope.

On December 22, 1899, Moody awoke to his last winter dawn and spoke slowly: "Earth recedes, heaven opens before me!" With his family around him, he went to be with the Lord.

Moody experienced the abundant life because of the power of Christ's resurrection. He not only enjoyed the life God gave him, but he knew even greater things were awaiting him when he died. For the Christian, death does not bring the end. We merely move from abundance to hyper-abundance, all because of the power of the resurrection of Christ. Jesus said, "I am the resurrection and the life. He who believes in me will live, even though he dies" (John 11:25, NIV).

God desires and has provided for each of us to enjoy an abundant life. That is truly what *living like Jesus* is about. Let us join with Paul and declare, "I want to know Christ and the power of his resurrection" (Philippians 3:10).

Eddy Brewer has been senior pastor of Abundant Life Assembly of God in Grapevine, Texas, from 1986 to the present. Brewer received his B.A. in religion from Dallas Baptist University and the M.S. in counseling from Texas A&M—Commerce in 1984. He has served at three churches in Dallas, Texas—in music, youth, and as an associate. Eddy and his wife, Claudia, have four children: Christy, Scott, Jamie, and Tiffany.

25

Grown Up

J.P. MCCAMEY

Spiritual growth is mentioned in 2 Peter 3:18: "But grow in the grace and knowledge of our Lord and Savior Jesus Christ" (NKJV). Ephesians 4:15 (Amplified) says, "Enfolded in love, let us *grow up* in every way and in all things into Him, Who is the Head, [even] Christ, the Messiah, the Anointed One."

When a child is acting childish, parents often say, "Grow up." It is an admonition children God frequently need as well. We need a lot of work. Paul said, "Now your attitudes and thoughts must all be constantly changing for the better" (Ephesians 4:23, LB). Quite an order. It sounds as if Paul is saying, "Go get a ladder and get over it." Most churches used to have attendance and offering boards up front. It is said that one read this way: Attendance, 312; Offering, $1,234; Feeling hurt, 35; Mad, 16.

We'll look at four admonitions that help Christians grow.

AVOID NEGATIVITY

To grow spiritually, Christians must avoid bad advice which can lead to a withering spirit. Why do some go for counseling to those who have failed miserably in their own lives? That's like a mosquito trying to suck blood out of a mummy. Christ is "the way and the truth and the life" (John 14:6, NIV). Those giving advice contrary to His teaching hinder spiritual growth.

A believer who is not growing up in the Lord must not blame others for their failure.

As one person said, "If that guy who sat next to me in high school had been smart, there's no telling what I might have become."

We need to pray, "Search me, O God, and know my heart: try me, and know my thoughts" (Psalm 139:23, KJV).

Is your spiritual growth stalled? Perhaps it is because of the tendency to look back at past failures and figure you just don't have what it takes to live successfully for Christ. Christians must not live in the "pastlane." As Paul said in Philippians 3:13, we must be "forgetting those things which are behind, and reaching forth unto those things which are before."

Someone who was consistently negative said, "I feel sure that, as a baby, my first step must have been backwards." This attitude can continue to affect one's life even into old age. It was said of an elderly person who had never gotten things straight spiritually, "He's 90 years old and still going wrong." How sad. Compare this with Job 17:9 (LB): "The righteous shall move onward and forward; those with pure hearts shall become stronger and stronger."

The word *solution* speaks most often of something that answers a question or problem; but to a chemist, the word *solution* means something that is all mixed up. Which sort of solution describes your life? Perhaps your mixed-up circumstances have caused your spiritual growth to be stunted. Certainly the most powerful hindrance is sin.

Someone has said, "Nature forms us, sin deforms us, education can inform us, the penitentiary might reform us, but only Christ can transform us."

"And be not conformed to this world: but be ye *transformed* by the renewing of your mind" (Romans 12:2, KJV). His transforming of your mind will break the power of sin and start you on your way to new spiritual growth.

FOLLOW CHRIST'S EXAMPLE

Here then is the key to growth in the Spirit—following Christ and His teaching. During war times, there have been those who knew the location of land mines placed underground in certain areas. Soldiers could follow them closely and avoid being blown to bits. There has to be an increasing desire to stay close to Jesus. He is the only one who can show us how to avoid all the spiritual land mines. The Amplified Bible renders the word "alive" (Romans 6:11) as "living in unbroken fellowship with Him."

At a time trail for the Indianapolis 500, I thought of this simplistic explanation of getting around the track: "Just keep going left and hurry back." There's a lot more to it than that, but that is essentially how one grows in Christ. Keep coming back to Him for strength and guidance. "Therefore also now, says the Lord, turn and *keep on coming to Me* with all your heart, with fasting, with weeping, and with mourning [until every hindrance is removed and the broken fellowship is restored]" (Joel 2:12, Amplified).

But too often, just as the Israelites rejected intimacy with God and urged Moses to stand in their place, so do God's people today. A deacon had a little boy who would go around the house singing, "Send Him on down, send Him on down, Lord, let the Holy Ghost come on down." Then he would launch into his own added version: "Take Him on up, take Him on up..." Perhaps Christians do that when the Lord is trying to bring them to a new depth of spiritual growth. It may be a tremendous service and the Holy Spirit is coming down in a powerful way. But because He strikes a sensitive hidden item in the heart which the individual is not willing to give up, that person in essence sings, "Take Him on up."

For achieving spiritual growth, there is no better life to emulate than that of our Lord. It was said of Him as a boy that He "grew in wisdom and stature, and in favor with God and men" (Luke 2:52, NIV).

GROW, as an acrostic, can stand for Go Right On Working (as opposed to GROSS, Go Right On Standing Still).

Mark 10:45 says of Jesus, "For even the Son of Man came not to be ministered unto, but to minister, and to give his life a ransom for many" (KJV). We all know that physically, we have to burn calories by activity and exercise. Just so, we grow spiritually by working for Him. That may involve church ministries, soul winning, and many other ways of performing His work.

In his book, *Keeping Pace,* Ernest Fitzgerald tells of wealthy English philanthropist, Jeremy Bentham. He had bequeathed a fortune to a London hospital on whose board of directors he had sat for decades. There was, though, one peculiar stipulation. Mr. Bentham's will read that in order for the hospital to keep the money, he Jeremy Bentham, had to be present at every board meetings. So for more than 100 years the cremated remains of Jeremy Bentham were brought to the board room every month and placed at the head of the table. And for more than 100 years the minutes of every meeting had a line that read, "Mr. Jeremy Bentham, present but not voting."

Many church people resemble Jeremy Bentham. They are present but not voting. They have good intentions but never seem to be growing spiritually. One reason is that they are not busy for Christ. The very act of reaching out to others causes growth.

The story is told of a man in a fierce blizzard who was about to give up. Unable to fight the storm any longer, he fell into the snow...onto something. It was another person. He quickly began to try to rub life back into the man's limbs since he was obviously about to freeze to death. He picked him up and stumbled onward. Then he saw the lights of a house and they both were saved.

What made the difference? As he focused his attention on helping another, he received the strength to go on. As we help others, we receive strength and grow in the Lord.

ABSORB GOD'S WORD

There is another method for growth that is essential: knowing, believing, and putting into practice the Word of God.

"As newborn babes, desire the sincere milk of the word, that ye may *grow* thereby" (1 Peter 2:2, KJV). The Amplified says, "That by it you may be nurtured and grow unto [completed] salvation." Acts 20:32 adds: "And now, brethren, I commend you to God, and to the *word* of his grace, which is able to *build you up*, and to give you an inheritance among all them which are sanctified" (KJV). His Word will do just that—build you up and help you to grow up.

Acts 19:20 is revealing: "So mightily grew the word of God and prevailed." Does it seem that you can't grow spiritually? Don't forget, as you get His Word in your heart and practice it by faith, it will prevail over all the enemy's devices. Then Satan might as well try to drown a fish as to sink you.

Jesus knew the Word and used it often. See how He overcame Satan three times with "It is written" (Matthew 4:4, 7, 10). Notice that He did not have to say, "Just a minute, devil; let me look it up in the concordance....I'll find something to use against you."

Obviously, Christ believed in His Father. He often spoke about faith. Can it be said of us what is found in 2 Thessalonians 1:3: "Your faith *groweth* exceedingly"? Remember that Jesus once addressed His disciples, "O ye of little faith" (Matthew 8:26). When we are going through stressful times, we are apt to rephrase it, "O *me* of little faith."

When does faith fail to grow? When we don't exercise it: "Faith without works is dead" (James 2:20). Also, faith erodes when we are not built up continually by His Word: "Faith cometh by hearing, and hearing by the word of God" (Romans 10:17, KJV). Conversely, it could also be said, "Faith *goeth* by *not* hearing the Word."

But there is another way to build faith. Faith (or faithfulness) is one of the nine fruit of the Holy Spirit (Galatians 5:22). If you are a Christian, you already have the Holy Spirit. "Now if any man have not the Spirit of Christ, he is none of his" (Romans 8:9). God drew you to himself by the Holy Spirit and lives by that Spirit in you. However, He wants to be not just a "resident" but also your "President."

It is important that your mind—that computer between your ears—be controlled by Him. When that happens, He will give you what you need to grow. As you surrender to Him, the Holy Spirit will take control. Along the way, you will then find that faith will increase along with the other fruit.

GIVE PRAISE TO GOD

Last, look at Abraham in Romans 4:20: "He *grew* strong and was *empowered by faith* as he gave praise and glory to God" (Amplified). You can do the same. Practice Psalm 34:1: "I will bless the Lord at all times [not 'except for when I don't feel good or when things are going against me']: his praise shall *continually* be in my mouth" (KJV). But how do you do that? "Seven times a day do I praise thee because of thy righteous judgments" (Psalm 119:164, KJV). Try it, perhaps at two-hour intervals; for example, 8 a.m., 10, 12, 2, 4, 6, 8. There are the seven times. A few minutes seven times a day, by a song of praise, a Scripture praising Him, or by going over some of the names of Christ. Do it when you're in line at the grocery store (it always seems to be the longest anyway) or when you're waiting in the doctor's office or in traffic.

Take time seven times a day to stop and praise Him. Abraham "grew strong and was empowered by faith" as he praised and gave glory to God. Try it. It will enhance your prayer life more than you can imagine.

You will grow spiritually. Avoid the negative, gloomy counselors. Move forward daily (not backward in doubt, fear, or worry). Look to Christ for your example and the power to grow as you work for Him, believing and practicing His Word and praising the Lord.

J.P. McCamey became a Christian at age 15. His first pastorate was in a home in McGregor, Texas, while he was in high school. He then attended Baylor University, Waco, Texas. McCamey served as assistant pastor at Calvary Assembly, Waco, Texas. He has been senior pastor at Assemblies of God churches in Midway, Texas; San Antonio, Texas; Stigler, Oklahoma; Fairview, Oklahoma; and Galena, Kansas. For 18 years he pastored First Assembly of God, Great Bend, Kansas.

While there, he launched a television ministry and oversaw four building programs, including a sanctuary to seat 1,200. McCamey has traveled in full-time evangelistic work since 1991. He has had more than 100 articles published in various publications, primarily the Pentecostal Evangel. *McCamey and his wife, Elsie, live in Bloomington, Indiana. They have one daughter, Debbie; and two sons, Jerry G., pastor of Calvary Temple in Indianapolis, Indiana; and Alan, general manager of New Horizons in Indianapolis. They have 11 grandchildren.*

26

Forgiveness as a Way of Life

DAVID A. GARCIA

Jesus said, "By this all will know that you are My disciples, if you have love for one another" (John 13:35, NKJV). The church needs to walk in love if we are to win the world for Jesus. Love means being determined to exercise our will to do whatever is needed to benefit the other person, regardless of how we feel. One of the most compelling examples of love is forgiveness.

What is forgiveness? How do we really forgive? Do I have to forget when I forgive? What are the consequences of unforgiveness? These and other questions will be answered by examining seven aspects of the words of Jesus in Matthew 18:22-35.

DIFFICULTY IN FORGIVING

"Then Peter came to him and said, 'Lord, how often shall my brother sin against me, and I forgive him? Up to seven times?'" (v. 21). Here are the basic reasons we find difficulty in forgiving.

Selfishness. Man is basically selfish and forgiveness is unselfish.

Self-righteousness. Often we don't forgive or ask forgiveness because we're too consumed by excuses: "I did not do anything wrong."

Pride. Pride is the opposite of mercy, and forgiveness is an act of mercy.

Emotional pain. Many can never get over the hurt inflicted upon them by another.

DECEPTION IN FORGIVING

"Jesus said to him, 'I do not say to you, up to seven times...'" (v. 22). In order to understand forgiveness, let's examine what is *not* forgiveness.

Forgiveness is not trying to ignore the hurt, agreeing with the hurt, only partial forgiveness, attaching conditions for reconciliation, or the lessening of anger over a period of time.

DEFINITION OF FORGIVENESS

Matthew 18:22 command us to forgive "up to seventy times seven." The following five powerful truths will not only define forgiveness but unlock the prison of bitterness and relieve the pain of being hurt.

Forgiveness is a realization. We must realize that Jesus died on Calvary as our substitute not only for our sins (what we did wrong) but also for our sorrows (what others did wrong to us). "He is despised and rejected by men, a *Man of sorrows* and acquainted with grief....Surely He has borne our griefs and *carried our sorrows...*" (Isaiah 53:3, 4). On Calvary, Jesus died for all my sins. I am free from the penalty of hell. Jesus also died for all my sorrows—the sins others committed *against me.*

I am free from the penalty of bitterness. Forgiveness, therefore, is *allowing* Jesus to carry my sorrows instead of *me* carrying them like luggage at an airport.

Forgiveness is receiving. I must receive the love and mercy of God and then make that love and mercy available to everyone who *wrongs* me.

Forgiveness is a replacement. We must replace resentment due to the inequities of life with the love and lordship of Jesus Christ and His Word. The key: Where will we focus? If our focus is on past hurts, we will become bitter. If on disappointment and disillusionment, we become irritable. If on unfair treatment or abuse, we become hateful. If our focus is on what Jesus accomplished, we forgive.

Forgiveness is releasing. We must release the offender from the sorrows and hurt that he has done to us, in obedience to Jesus, as well as releasing mercy and love to him as Jesus did to us.

Forgiveness is remembrance. Contrary to the popular belief of forgive and forget, God does not give us divine amnesia. Rather, we are to remember the offense without the pain of the offense which will enable us to help, minister, and relate to others with similar hurts. The world cries, "You have no idea what I've been through." We can say in return, "I know how you feel. Been there; done that. But Jesus took my pain away and He can do the same for you."

DESCRIPTION OF FORGIVENESS

Let's look at four descriptions of forgiveness from Jesus' parable in Matthew 18:23-27.

Pay day. "Therefore the kingdom of heaven is like a certain king who wanted to settle accounts with his servants" (v. 23). This teaches us that we all will give account of our lives to Jesus. In life, we all eventually offend others or will be asked by others for forgiveness.

Payment. "And when he had begun to settle accounts, one was brought to him who owed him ten thousand talents. But as he was not able to pay, his master commanded that he be sold, with his wife and children and all that he had, and that payment be made" (vv. 24-25). This servant owed him approximately $1 million and could not possibly pay; therefore, he was facing slavery for himself and his family.

Plea. "The servant therefore fee down before him, saying, 'Master, have patience with me, and I will pay you all'" (v. 26). The servant asked for an extension of time in order to make the payments. Patience is the Greek word *makrothumeo* indicating extension of time, not release from obligation.

Pardon. "Then the master of that servant was moved with compassion, released him, and forgave him the debt" (v. 27). The servant no longer owed anything.

DENIAL OF FORGIVENESS

"But that servant went out and found one of his fellow servants who owed him a hundred denarii [about 100 days' wages]; and he laid hands on him and took him by the throat, saying, 'Pay me what you owe!' So his fellow servant fell down at his feet and begged him, saying, 'Have patience with me, and I will pay you all.' And he would not, but went and threw him into prison till he should pay the debt" (vv. 28-30).

We see six unfortunate factors:

Inquiry. This forgiven servant does not appreciate or understand that he has been forgiven an insurmountable debt because he asked for an extension yet received total pardon. He acts like many Christians who must do a righteous act or punish themselves for the wrong they've done. He could not accept his own forgiveness; therefore, he makes others miserable.

Indebtedness. What is $100 compared to $1 million?

Ire. There is bitterness in many Christians instead of forgiveness.

Invocation. Note that his servant also asked for an extension to make the payments but was denied.

Insensitivity. Why do we deny forgiveness to others when we have received Christ's forgiveness?

Imprisonment. We too can sentence people to coldness, indifference, hatred, and bitterness.

DEMAND FOR FORGIVENESS

"So when his fellow servants saw what had been done, they were very grieved, and came and told their master all that had been done" (v. 31). We see four things here about unforgiveness: Unforgiveness will be *recognized, reacted to, reported,* and *reaped.* "And his master was angry, and delivered him to the torturers until he should pay all that was due to him" (v. 34).

DISASTER OF NOT FORGIVING

"Then his master, after he had called him, said to him, 'You wicked servant! I forgave you all that debt because you begged me. Should you not also have had compassion on your fellow servant, just as I had pity on you?' And his master was angry, and delivered him to the torturers until he should pay all that was due to him. So My heavenly Father also will do to you if each of you, from his heart, does not forgive his brother his trespasses" (vv. 32-35).

Here are four consequences of unforgiveness: He is *categorized* as a wicked servant; he is *chastised* for not extending the same privilege of forgiveness that he himself received; he is *condemned.*

In addition, we are *cautioned* that the Father will turn Christians over to oppression if they do not forgive.

Many Christians are tormented physically, emotionally, and mentally because of unforgiveness.

How then do we forgive?

STEPS IN FORGIVENESS

We must forgive them out of a desire to please Jesus as our Lord. We must forgive as an act of faith rather than from feelings. "For we walk by faith, not by sight" (2 Corinthians 5:7). In other words, faith moves with a conviction to forgive in the fear of the Lord and in obedience to His Word despite personal offense or emotions. We must walk and make decisions by faith and in the Spirit—but never by feelings. Use the "forgive by faith" method. Hebrews 11:1 says, "Now faith is the substance of things hoped for, the evidence of things not seen." Let's paraphrase this verse to specifically apply to forgiveness: "Now faith is the forgiveness that I hope for, the evidence of which I do not see in me." Realize that when we allow our soul (mind, emotions, and will) to dominate our decision, the soul is basically self-centered and in itself may decide against forgiveness.

Our mind says, "I can't forget what they did to me." Our emotions say, "I'm hurt. I'm offended." Our will says, "I will not forgive. I sentence you to be the object of my indifference or bitterness."

You must choose instead to walk in the Spirit (Galatians 5:16); that is, to allow your human spirit, empowered by the Holy Spirit, to make the decision to forgive. How? By considering the soul of Jesus. His mind said, "I died for your sins and your sorrows" (Isaiah 53:3-4, paraphrased). His emotions said, "I am grieved that you ask for forgiveness for yourself but do not forgive others" (paraphrased, see Matthew 6:12). His will said, "Forgive them for it is not my will but yours that matters" (Matthew 26:39, paraphrased).

We must continue to live in repentance and forgiveness. This can be accomplished by following six biblical directives:

- Seek God daily in love and worship (Matthew 22:37).
- Confess and repent of your sins (John 16:8).
- Realize that offenses are an opportunity to portray a good witness for Christ.
- Prevent a "root of bitterness" (Hebrews 12:15) from developing in you by forgiving the offender or asking to be forgiven at the moment of the offense. Never allow the other person's spirit to be wounded because this leads to bitterness (Proverbs 18:14).
- Be quick to ask for and offer forgiveness, even without the expectation that you will be forgiven or that the other person will ask you to forgive them. Expect nothing in return but the pleasure of the Lord (Psalm 62:5).
- Remember that every offense and conflict will prepare and enable you to better minister to others. The world says, "Seeing is believing" and "You don't understand what I've been through." You will be able to say, "I know what you feel. I've been there, but I no longer have the pain." When they ask why and how, share what Jesus has done for you.

Let's walk in love and forgiveness, the way that Jesus walked. Remember, the greatest sermon someone may ever experience is your asking for or offering forgiveness.

David A. Garcia has served as senior pastor of the fast-growing Brooksville Assembly of God in Brooksville, Florida, since 1988. Garcia has been a missionary in Zimbabwe,

Africa; and in New Your City. He formerly served as the singles ministry coordinator of the Peninsular Florida District of the Assemblies of God and is an assistant presbyter. He is the author of Equipped to Include, *part of the* We Build People *discipleship series. A popular speaker at seminars, camps, and conferences, he has conducted overseas pastors seminars and evangelistic crusades. He and his wife, Nellie, have two children: Carissa and David.*

27

Click Here

NORMAN LAWRENCE

The 1900s brought changes that have made our lives more comfortable. Automobiles, airplanes, vacuum cleaners, dishwashers, television, microwaves, air conditioners, catalytic converters, fax machines, washers and dryers, ballpoint pens, MRIs, and a host of other 20th-century inventions have helped streamline nearly every move. One of the most significant inventions was the computer. The Internet has opened up a vast frontier—and has presented new challenges to followers of Jesus Christ.

This chapter will address the mounting challenges believers face in this day of runaway technology.

WHO USES THE INTERNET?

People from all walks of life are surfing the Net. What used to be reserved for government agencies and computer geeks is now being used by people of all ages for research; conferencing; banking; e-mail; retrieving survey information; and E-commerce, the online equivalent of brick-and-mortar department stores.

Ministries are realizing the benefits of having their information on the Internet as well. Churches are able to post pictures of their facilities, display their vision statements, post events on an online calendar, even upload the plan of salvation with a feedback form for use of those making decisions for Christ. People moving into a new area can go online and search for churches in the particular area to which they have moved. They can browse through the various church Web sites. It is not only neat but necessary for a church to have a Web site for its people to view. The church Web site should be considered an online visitor packet, enabling browsers to "visit" the church from their home or office computer to become more familiar with the various ministries before making a visit to the church building.

Evangelistic ministries as well are finding tremendous benefits in placing their information online with their itinerary, mission statements, travel arrangements, preaching and singing audio clips, online forms for feedback, and more.

The benefits provided by the Internet to pastors, teachers, and others in presenting the Word of God also are tremendous.

What would take hours of leafing through pages of books in limited personal and community libraries can now often be discovered in moments with a focused search on the Internet.

WHAT'S THE PROBLEM?

Jesus said, "Go into all the world." The Internet can be a powerful tool if put to work to fulfill the Great Commission. The Christian can make a difference on the Internet. However, they must also be aware of the dangers. It cannot be left to the world to make it a *Worldly* Wide Web.

The tempter has always assaulted believers. The Internet is no exception. This superhighway is littered with potholes, roadblocks, and detours that have driven many Christians away from their eternal goal.

When Jesus was here on earth, Satan tempted Him in the three areas identified in 1 John 2:16: "For all that is in the world, the lust of the flesh, and the lust of the eyes, and the pride of life, is not of the Father, but is of the world" (KJV). The lust of the flesh is temptation to gratify physical desires. The lust of the eyes deals with the accumulation of things. The pride of life focuses on the realm of one's status. Our focus will be on the most obvious problem area on the Internet, the lust of the flesh.

In much the same way, the Internet has become the stone that can be turned to bread for many Christians.

In Matthew 4 Jesus is being tempted in the wilderness. "After fasting forty days and forty nights, he was hungry" (v. 2, NIV). Hunger is a natural, God-given need placed within each of us for the primary purpose of sustaining life. Enjoyment is derived from satisfying that hunger.

The enemy knew that after 40 days in the wilderness abstaining from food, Christ would be hungry. "The tempter came to him and said, 'If you are the Son of God, tell these stones to become bread'" (v. 3). Satan was focusing on a perfectly normal desire, attempting to pervert it to get Christ to detour from the path He was now on. Christ was physically weak following the 40 days of fasting, and Satan knew this would be the time to take advantage of the situation. Jesus knew that to turn the stones into bread was not God the Father's way nor was it the right time to satisfy His hunger. The temptation came from the enemy to Christ to gratify *right desires* in a *wrong way* and at the *wrong time*.

The trap of pornography has been opened wide to Christians who have allowed the enemy to have a foothold as they surf. Satan's challenge today may no longer be "turn these stones into bread." The words the enemy uses today may go something like this: click here. Anonymity, affordability, and availability are three characteristics of the Internet. These three factors are ingredients for danger for the spiritually weak person. Christ, though weak physically, had been in prayer and fellowship with the Father and was able to withstand the attack of the enemy through that strength and the Word of God.

The anonymity factor is up for debate; but for the person alone with a computer in home or office, there is a feeling of being alone with the world at one's fingertips. One of the ploys of the enemy is, "No one will ever know. It will be just our secret."

Internet access is affordable to the vast majority of users. In fact, it is available for free in much of the United States. But there is a catch. Surfers must view banner advertisements with "click here" messages. Furious battles have raged in the inner recesses of the heart with the open combat played out by the movements of a little device called a mouse. Just a click will lead the user to the worst the world has to offer.

During the 1980s, there was a noted decline in pornography in America. In 1986, the attorney general made recommendations concerning its regulation, and many of those recommendations made their way into law. Cyberspace, however, has presented new challenges to those who are entrusted with enforcing these laws. Now there is an endless supply of pornography available right on the computer screen in the privacy of one's own home or place of employment. Many companies have been to track their employees' usage. Tragically, many have lost their job, reputation, and at times their family due to these activities.

The porn industry is recruiting thousands of viewers who otherwise would not even step on the property of an adult bookstore. The porn industry knows there is a powerful addiction associated with its usage and that online use will frequently be carried over into other establishments as well. According to a *U.S. News and World Report* article, the porn industry took in more than $8 billion in one year—"more than all revenues generated by rock and country music, and more than America spent on Broadway productions, theater, ballet, jazz, and classical music combined." According to a report by CNET.com (April 1999), it was estimated that there were quite possibly 7 million X-rated sites on the Net at the time. The same report also suggests that up to 30 million people log onto pornographic Web sites every day. The usage has undoubtedly climbed since then.

WHAT TO DO?

With all the temptations that enter our homes via Internet access, one might ask if it is even worthwhile for a Christian to be online.

The benefits far outweigh the negatives, but one must be constantly mindful of the dangers and know how to avoid a spiritual crash on the superhighway.

Following are some steps that will help believers deal with temptation as Jesus would:

1. *Pray for God's guidance and strength as you navigate the Net.* When Jesus was in the wilderness for 40 days, He fasted and prayed. The strength He drew from this communion clearly assisted Him in His test.

2. *Harbor the Word in your heart.* Jesus used the Word of God to thwart the attack of the enemy. The Bible is available in many different forms today, such as print, CDs, computer program, and online. However, there is no substitute for the Word written on your heart.

3. *Be accountable.* Have your computer in a position so the screen can be easily viewed by anyone walking by. Do not allow it in your child's bedroom. Share your email password with your spouse and be open to their reading your email anytime.

4. *Purchase filtering software,* especially when children can go online while parents are not at home. This software will filter out much of the filth. An excellent free source of filtering (as of this writing) is found at www.weblocker.com.

5. *Be educated.* One of the tragedies is for parents to be at the mercy of their children when it comes to computer issues. Don't assume new tricks can't be taught to an old dog. This issue is too important for parents to simply ignore.

6. *Examine your heart.* In using a financial program on my home computer, the file name I use is simply "Family." As I begin doing backups of the data to ensure it would be elsewhere in case of system failure, these words come up on the screen while the process is taking place: "Backing Up 'Family.'" Every time I see those words (as well as other times), I ask myself if what I am doing on this computer is "backing up my family." May nothing we do be detrimental to our families.

7. *Develop a Web site.* You can make a difference on the Web by learning some design techniques. Various software programs make it a snap to

design a site. Churches are often in need of just the right person to volunteer their services to develop a quality Web site.

8. *Just say no.* When temptation comes, do not even entertain the thought. Resist the rationale that becoming educated about the things that are available online will make you better equipped to warn others. This information is better garnered from those who have done the research rather than by firsthand experience.

Immeasurable damage has been inflicted upon families because men and women have yielded to the temptation to turn stones into bread and satisfy their God-given desires in the wrong way at the wrong time.

Approach the Internet as Jesus would and use the tools that God has given for His glory and honor, not for self-gratification.

Norman Lawrence graduated from Zion Bible Institute, Barrington, Rhode Island, in 1982 and has been in full-time ministry since, serving churches in West Virginia and Pennsylvania as youth pastor and pastor, and since 1995, as associate pastor at Peckville Assembly of God, Peckville, Pennsylvania. He and his wife, Brenda, have recorded an album, One Less Stone. *Lawrence is the trademark owner and distributor of an inspirational gift product,* Quiet Stones. *He also designs Web sites with his company,* Designs for Ministry. *Lawrence believes that the Internet can be a tool for ministries to share information and to spread the gospel. He and Brenda have two children: Dwayne and Aaron.*

www.BidforJesus.com

RANDY JUMPER

I have only done it once. I will never do it again.

As a budding 21st-century information-age junkie, I am hooked on the Internet and the idea that bargain prices are available on anything if you find the right Web site. In this never-ending and typically fruitless quest (don't tell my wife; she thinks I'm saving money), I logged on to a discount travel site. The site promises super-savings on travel costs by letting people name their own price for airfare and hotels. Cheapskates like me drool at the opportunity to save hundreds of dollars, and this was no exception. After you name your price and class of service, they match you with a hotel. When my wife and I needed a room, I satisfied my relentless desire for a better deal by trying the discount route. After viewing the options, I picked a three-star hotel and then bid a very low price.

Within an hour, they found a "three-star hotel" that accepted my price. I called my wife, reveling in the $30-40 I had saved because I named my price. She was skeptical.

When the trip came, the bargain hotel excited me more than the rest of the trip. I could not wait to get to our room. When we arrived, I opened the door and confidently marched into my "mansion" of a hotel room. Within seconds, my wife said, "You get what you pay for." She was right. My dream hotel at budget prices did not exist.

After picking up the pieces of my ego, I tried to find what went wrong. I did exactly what the company said to do, but my room was not the high-class suite I expected. The more I thought about it, I realized how heavily I was influenced by the lie that infects our culture: Success is investing the minimum amount—name your own price— and getting the maximum results. We constantly find ways to decrease the energy, money, and time we spend expecting to increase productivity.

This concept affects spiritual lives as well. Christians expect God to give all He promised while we give Him as little as possible. How many times have we tried to name our own price for His blessings? "Jesus, if You help me financially, I will change the way I spend my money," or "If You save me out of this situation, I will never do it again." We log on www.BidforJesus.com* and name our own price for being His disciple. We set the limit of commitment expecting the same benefits, if not more. We lack the primary ingredient of living like Jesus in the 21st-century—surrender.

The struggle of surrender is not new. The rich young ruler in Luke 18 also struggled. He came to Christ seeking eternal life with a limit on what he would give in return. He came to Jesus naming his own price, and Jesus responded with a series of challenges that shook the foundation of the man's search. Unable to accept Christ's challenge, he walked away sadly.

From the beginning, the ruler seems out of place. Jesus usually ministered to the poor, sick, and oppressed. Men of wealth rarely came to Jesus. Yet nestled between the stories of blind men, lepers, and children, a rich, educated ruler appears. Why would *he* come? Jesus' disciples must have looked in wonder at the appearance of aristocracy before the poor prophet from Nazareth. The man with everything—power, money, and education—had come seeking life. His words ring with dissatisfaction and lack of fulfillment. Sadly, the ruler never got past the sense of dissatisfaction. Jesus challenged him, but he wanted to name his own price.

In this book, you will find many different aspects of living like Jesus. But before you can be like Jesus, you must first follow Jesus.

Following Christ as His disciple leads to the greatest sense of fulfillment a person can have. It begins in surrendering to Him and His lordship—not dictating how you will follow Him. There is no room in God's kingdom for www. BidforJesus.com.

In this story, Jesus reveals the important first steps of surrendering to Christ through three challenges to the ruler. These steps determine the rest of the path of discipleship. Surrender is difficult, but the reward is worth the sacrifice. Taking these steps means we quit naming our price to be His disciple.

CHECK YOUR FOCUS

Jesus' first words to the ruler are a challenge for all of us: "Why do you call me good?" (v. 19, NIV). Jesus knew the man had not come with the right attitude. He had come to Jesus, but his focus was on himself: "What must *I* do to inherit eternal life?...All these I have kept since I was a boy" (vv. 18, 21). Jesus knew the rich young ruler assumed he could achieve eternal life through his own effort. This distorted his perception of Jesus and prevented him from finding the answer. Jesus wanted to know who he really thought was good—Jesus or himself. The first step of surrender is to focus on Christ and not ourselves.

Compare the young ruler with the Roman centurion of Matthew 8:5-13. The centurion came to Jesus seeking healing for his servant. In humility, he acknowledged he was not worthy to have Jesus in his home. Focused on Christ, not himself, he called Jesus *Lord* while the ruler called Jesus *teacher*. He was willing to do anything for the healing of his servant. Jesus said that the centurion's faith was like no other's in Israel. How ironic that a Jewish ruler could miss the truth understood by this Gentile soldier. Each came to Jesus, but only the centurion received the answer.

Before we judge the ruler, we must examine our own lives. We all are tempted to name our own price at times. We try to do enough good things to get what we want from God.

The young ruler did this in trying to keep the law. Like him, we can keep score with our faith, hoping that at the end of each week, we will have given the least to get the most from God. I call this collecting God points. "Let's see, I read my Bible four times this week; that's eight points. Attended church twice; that's 10 points. I need God to provide for the new car my family needs, so I'll give $25 to missions on Sunday; that plus tithe equals 20 points. I didn't use profanity and said no to the guys at work who went to the bar; that's 50 points. That's 88 God points which is enough to get me through next week—when I skip church to go skiing—and still have God help us financially with the car."

God points become our bargaining chips used to force God to accept the price we name. "God, I did x, y, and z, so you *must* work a miracle in my life." We set the parameters of commitment. The focus is on us, not on Christ. We name what we will give to be His disciple. Do we come focused on Christ or ourselves? Jesus challenges us, "Why do you call Me good? Why do you even come to Me for answers?"

CLEAR AWAY BARRIERS

Jesus' next challenge cut to the core of the ruler's problem. He responded to the ruler's question by reminding him of the law. The ruler answered, "All these I have kept" (v. 21). Jesus doesn't argue whether or not he kept the commandments; this was not His point. "You still lack one thing," Jesus said (v. 22). The ruler did a lot of things right, but they were not enough. The second step of surrender is clearing away the barriers preventing you from following Christ.

Jesus asked the young ruler to surrender the wealth that gave him his identity (after all, we know him only as the *rich* young ruler). Imagine Jesus asking you to surrender the thing that sets you apart and makes you significant. Who we are must be lost in who Christ is. In Galatians 2:20, Paul summarizes this: "Not I, but Christ" (KJV). It is Christ who gives us life, not anything we do.

The price for following Jesus was a high one. For the young ruler, his money was more important than surrendering to Christ.

He wanted eternal life, but he wanted to name his own price.

Placing myself in the role of the younger ruler, I know if Jesus confronted me, He wouldn't say, "*One* thing you lack." It would sound more like, "These 47 things you lack." We all have things that hinder us from surrendering. The good things we accomplish in life are nothing if something hinders our complete commitment.

All our works—teaching Sunday school, holy living, or giving—are worthless when something blocks our surrender. We, like the young ruler, are so proud of what we do right that we do not see what we do wrong.

If you met Jesus today, what would He find lacking in you? What is Jesus asking you to give up? Is He asking you to remember the poor more often than holidays? Is He asking you to give up promotion at work for spiritual growth? Is He asking you to give personal time to work with children at church? Are there unconfessed sins in your life? What prevents you from complete surrender to Christ? Do not walk away sadly; do not name your own price. Clear away the barriers to surrendering to Christ.

COMMIT TO BEING A FLLOWER

Jesus' final words to the rich young ruler demanded a response. Jesus challenged several with these imperatives: "Come, follow me" (v. 22, NIV). They summarize the life of discipleship and echo through time even today. The final step of surrender is following after Christ.

To complete this step, we must come to Christ. It is an active work on our part. We stop what we are doing and move. This is our decision; Jesus does not force us to begin the journey of discipleship. Before we can follow Him, we must first come to Him. The rich young ruler walked away.

Next, we follow Christ's leadership. Jesus did not ask the rich young ruler to join Him. He asked him to follow. Following Jesus gives protection and confidence that we are not alone. We see the road ahead as well as our Lord leading us. His presence comforts us through hard times and His strength sustains us as we journey. We join the centurion in calling Jesus Lord, surrendering everything to Him for a lifetime. While the journey has a definite beginning ("come"), following has no end.

The rich young ruler wanted eternal life on his own terms. He would not pay the price for following Jesus. Jesus was not interested in followers who would bid what they would give. Though Jesus takes us just as we are, the attitude of "take me as I am" has no room for the followers of Christ.

To surrender to Christ, first we check our focus—is it on Him or ourselves? Second, we must clear our lives of the barriers that hinder us from being His disciple. Third, we must commit to follow Him, no matter the cost. For centuries, men and women have been trying to name their own price in following Jesus while Jesus paid the real price with His death on Calvary's cross. We could not pay that price even if we named it.

Jesus bids, "Come, follow Me." You cannot name your price. The debt has already been paid—paid in full.

*Fictitious name

Randy Jumper and his wife, Heidi, are evangelists from Springfield, Missouri. In 1998, Jumper founded Compass Enterprises, an organization dedicated to leading lost people in the right direction. Randy received a B.A. from Central Bible College, Springfield, Missouri, and an M.Div. from Assemblies of God Theological Seminary. He currently serves as the assistant to the evangelists representative for the Assemblies of God where he works with denominational leaders developing resources for evangelism. The Jumpers also work in student development at Evangel University, Springfield, Missouri, coordinating the spiritual and social development of more than 200 students.

29

Serving in the Local Church

MIKE ENNIS

Author John Maxwell says there are three signs of a healthy church: people receiving Christ as Savior, laypeople involved in ministry, and laypeople answering the call for full-time ministry. On the other hand, one of the greatest threats to the local church is the unfulfilled potential of its constituency—when Christians are content to merely exist without working and living for Christ.

Matthew 20:26-28 commands us to look for opportunities to serve: "Whoever wants to become great among you must be your servant, and whoever wants to be first must be your slave—just as the Son of Man did not come to be served" (NIV). There are untold blessings for individuals and marvelous benefits to the kingdom of God when laypeople are empowered by their pastor and realize their servant potential.

THE ENABLER

The pastor's primary responsibility is to equip believers for the work of the ministry (Ephesians 4:11-12). Unfortunately, many of the ministry needs in the local church are perceived as undesirable chores rather than opportunities to invest in the lives of others. Some believers have become narcissistic, routinely dismissing ministry opportunities in the church in favor of serving themselves.

The Great Commission in Matthew 28 encourages believers to view every opportunity as a chance to demonstrate the love of Christ to a lost and dying world: seasonal dramas, community outreaches, compassion initiatives, Sunday morning ministries, and more. Every task, regardless of how important or unimportant it may seem, is an opportunity to touch others.

As your pastor equips you and provides opportunities for service, allow the Lord to propel you into His ministry. Your availability and dedication are an encouragement to your pastor and an act of service to your Savior.

THE EMPOWERER

Just as the pastor's role is to enable ministry, it is the congregation's role to empower the pastor and the church by offering their talents. By offering your God-given gifts to the church, you empower your pastor and your congregation as a whole. Jesus ordained pastors and the church. He wants the local church to thrive.

When you care about the things Jesus cares about and respond to needs as Jesus would respond, then you are following in the footsteps of Christ.

It pleases Him when you invest in your local church.

There are many vital ministries in the local church, and there are unlimited opportunities awaiting Christians who are willing to offer their talents for the Lord's work. There is a place for everyone to serve: music, drama, maintenance, visitation, teaching, and more.

There are also opportunities to minister in the community as an outreach of the church.

What ministries could be started in your church to reach out to unbelievers? A divorce recovery workshop? A home for unwed mothers? A food pantry? When the congregation gets involved in ministry—inside or outside the walls of the church—it empowers the local church to fulfill its mission.

There is a powerful trend toward compassion ministries in churches today. Believers are learning that everyone can do something to help people in need. And they're finding tremendous fulfillment in offering a cup of water or blanket in Jesus' name. One pastor who hosted a Convoy of Hope outreach (food distribution, medical screening, and job fair) in his community said it changed his church in a single day. What was once an introverted congregation is now a thriving, caring body of believers. Veteran Christians have also seen their lives changed. The congregation has moved outside the church walls and into the community.

If you feel called to offer your talents to a ministry of the church, share your heart with your pastor. Express your desire to dedicate your God-given talents and ask where there is a need you can meet.

Pray for the guidance of the Holy Spirit. Ask the Spirit to give you a burden for a particular ministry. He may want you to assist someone else or use you to establish a compassion ministry. Just be open to His leading.

Some servants become discouraged when they assume responsibility for a ministry but lack the knowledge or tools to complete the task. Ask yourself, *Is there a book I can read, a CD I can listen to, a conference I can attend, or a person who can mentor me?* Ensure your success in your area of ministry through education and spiritual preparation (e.g., prayer, Bible reading, and reliance on the Holy Spirit).

Serving Jesus in the local church can be one of the most rewarding experiences of your life. The partnership between the pastor and congregation to do the work of the ministry advances the kingdom of God and fulfills the church's mission. But it all begins with people who are willing to follow Christ's example into a life of servanthood.

Mike Ennis is executive vice president of Convoy of Hope, an organization that equips and mobilizes laity to reach hurting families in America's urban centers with groceries, medical assistance and dental screenings, job fairs, haircuts, and the gospel of Christ. He was senior associate pastor in Atlanta, Georgia, for 14 years. He coordinated the evangelism efforts for the 1996 Summer Olympic Games which facilitated the ministry of thousands of volunteers. Ennis lives in Springfield, Missouri, with his wife, Christy, and their sons: Christopher and Caleb.

30

Just Like Jesus Said

STEVEN DONALDSON

Jesus said the poor would be with us always. Indeed, this age of prosperity and technological advance, poverty continues to grow—at an alarming rate. Of the world's 6 billion people, 2.8 billion live on less than $2 a day; 1.2 billion on less than $1. In developing countries, as many as 50 percent of children are malnourished.[1] And 30 percent of the world's population lives in the least-developed countries and earns less than 1 percent of the world's income.[2] There is no end in sight for world poverty. In the next 25 years, an estimated 2 billion people will be added to the planet's population—mostly in developing countries.[3]

So how should Christ's followers respond to this massive challenge? Jesus taught that each person is created in the image of God and is therefore of immeasurable worth. Thus we must do everything possible to save lives on earth and for eternity.

In Luke 10:27, Jesus says, "Love the Lord your God with all your heart" and "Love your neighbor as yourself." This is a blueprint for nurturing relationships with God and others. Christians need to be others-minded and consider living simply so that others may simply live. We cannot live just for ourselves. When persons are already vulnerable because of poverty and then face a natural or man-made disaster, there is no safety net. They often succumb to disease and malnutrition. There is no insurance policy or welfare system to rescue them. The compassion of Christ demonstrated through us may be the only safety net they have.

Luke 3 demonstrates the importance of meeting practical, tangible needs. Jesus had just been baptized and the multitude had repented of their sins. They came to John the Baptist and asked, "What should we do [with this newfound faith in Jesus Christ]?" (v. 10).

John replied, "The man with two tunics should share with him who has none, and the one who has food should do the same" (v. 11).

As I sat in a restaurant in an impoverished country, street children came up to the window begging for food. The waiter promptly pulled down the shade. "Don't worry; they will go away," he said. Christ's followers cannot pull down the shades. We must lift them so we can clearly see how God might want to use us to touch some of His creations.

So what is our Christian responsibility to the hungry around the world? We must respond to their cries wherever and however possible.

In many situations around the world, a gift of food opens a door for the gospel of Jesus to be shared. An African proverb says it well: "An empty stomach has no ears." In many cases we must first feed a stomach before we can minister to a heart.

When Jesus performed the miracle of feeding the 5,000, He had the disciples collect the unused food, thereby demonstrating the importance of not wasting surplus. The United States of America has been blessed with a seemingly limitless food supply. More than 96 billion pounds of food every year are tossed or plowed underground. Agencies like Second Harvest and ministries like Convoy of Hope collect some of the surplus and distribute to people in need.

Many families in need are believers. Daily they cry out, "Jesus, provide our daily bread. Give us the bare necessities or a way to provide for our family." Is Jesus going to send a raven to feed them or manna from heaven? Probably not—instead He's sending you and me.

Scripture is given that "the man of God may be thoroughly equipped for every good work" (2 Timothy 3:17). The opportunity to respond to the destitute and dying must be seen as an open door. God has placed all the resources and giftedness necessary within His body of believers to rescue people for eternity. Of course, there continues to be a great need for preaching. But there is also need for people to respond to water shortages, inadequate shelter, poor sanitation, hunger, and the lack of economic development. You might say, "I want to help, but I don't have much." Jesus says that all it takes to start is to give a cup of cold water in His name.

Matthew 6:3 says, "But when you give to the needy, do not let your left hand know what your right hand is doing." What does this mean? There is very little my right hand is involved in that my left hand does not know. Could it be that Jesus is teaching that our good deeds should be so commonplace that we hardly notice?

The Old Testament recounts that God redeemed Israel out of the hands of the Egyptians and instructed them to assist people in need. In turn He promised His blessing: "Remember that you were slaves in Egypt and the Lord your God redeemed you from there. That is why I command you to do this. When you are harvesting in your field and you overlook a sheaf, do not go back to get it. Leave it for the alien, the fatherless and the widow, so that the Lord your God may bless you in all the work of your hands" (Deuteronomy 24:18-19). Proverbs 19:17 adds, "He who is kind to the poor lends to the Lord, and he will reward him for what he has done."

The New Testament perspective is found in Luke 12:48: "From everyone who has been given much, much will be demanded; and from the one who has been entrusted with much, much more will be asked."

We live in a nation of plenty. Abraham Lincoln said, "We have been recipients of the choicest bounties of heaven." We have been given much; thus, Jesus requires much from us. If we pursue opportunities to share out of our abundance, the lives of millions will be changed and churches will grow.

"A gift opens the way for the giver and ushers him into the presence of the great," says Proverbs 18:16. Albania, a country once restrictive to Christianity, permitted Convoy of Hope and other humanitarian groups to assist refugees fleeing Kosovo. Christian Albanians extended their helping hands to Islamic Kosovars, opening their homes and sharing their resources. When many of the refugees returned to Kosovo, the president of Albania claimed that one-tenth of one percent of the country was Christian. That small number of Christians had taken care of 15 percent of the refugees. This heroic expression of love has helped establish the Christian church in Kosovo. The sacrificial gifts of home, food, and life opened the hearts of many Kosovars to the gospel of Jesus Christ.

I have traveled to more than 30 countries and witnessed much suffering, but I have also experienced immense sacrificial love and practical expressions of Jesus to a troubled would. Jesus was asked by John the Baptist, "Are you the one who was to come, or should we expect someone else?" (Matthew 11:3). Jesus said, "The blind receive sight, the lame walk, those who have leprosy are cured, the deaf hear, the dead are raised, and the good news is preached to the poor" (v. 5). If I were asked what proves that I am a disciple of Christ, I hope I could respond, "Because my heart is broken with the things that break the heart of God."

Steven Donaldson is executive vice president of Convoy of Hope, a Christian humanitarian organization that equips and mobilizes churches and other agencies in the United States and around the world to provide physical and spiritual assistance to those in destitute areas or devastated by disaster. Donaldson was a senior pastor in California and is known for his compassion for the needy and his passion to motivate others to reach them. He lives in Springfield, Missouri, with his wife, Rebecca, and their sons: Joshua, Jordan, and Bryant.

ENDNOTES

INTRODUCTION
1. Isaiah 53:3 (NKJV)
2. Matthew 26:39
3. John 18:12-13
4. Matthew 26:57-68
5. John 18:15-27
6. Matthew 27:1
7. Matthew 27:5
8. Luke 23:1-4
9. Luke 23:6-11
10. Mark 15:6-15; Luke 23:13-25, paraphrased
11. Matthew 27:27-30; see also Philippians 2:9-11
12. See John 10:17-18
13. Matthew 27:31
14. John 19:16-17
15. Philippians 2:8
16. Luke 23:34
17. From "Beneath the Cross of Jesus" by E.C. Clephane and F.C. Maker
18. See Luke 9:23

CHAPTER 3
1. Dietrich Bonhoeffer, *Life Together*, trans. John W. Doberstein (New York: Harper & Brothers, 1954), 8.
2. Leon Morris, *The Gospel According to St. Luke*. The Tyndale New Testament Commentaries (Grand Rapids: Wm. B. Eerdmans Publishing Company, 1974), 180.
3. A. M. Hunter, *Interpreting the Parables* (London, 1960), 65.

CHAPTER 5
1. William Barclay, *The Gospel of Matthew,* vol. 2 (Philadelphia: Westminster, 1975), 317.

CHAPTER 9
1. Stephen Covey, *First Things First* (New York: Simon and Schuster, 1994), 88-89.

CHAPTER 10
1. Paul A. Cedar, *Strength in Servant Leadership* (Waco: Word Books, 1987), 150.

CHAPTER 19
1. Jim Cymbala, *Fresh Faith* (Grand Rapids: Zondervan, 1999), 16.

CHAPTER 21
1. *Leadership*, vol. 5, no. 1.
2. "The New Philanthropy," *Time*, July 24, 2000.
3. T.W. Manson, *Saying*, 261.
4. "Family Concern," *Christianity Today*, vol. 29, no. 17.

CHAPTER 30
1. World Development Report
2. Harvard International Review
3. World Development Report

ABOUT THE EDITORS

Ken Horn, D.Min., is managing editor of the *Pentecostal Evangel* in Springfield, Missouri. He received his bachelor's degree from Bethany College of the Assemblies of God, M.A. from Simpson College, D.Min. from California Graduate School of Theology, and did additional graduate work at Golden Gate Baptist Theological Seminary. Horn pastored three churches in California and Oregon. He has taught theology and related subjects on the graduate and undergraduate levels at Simpson College and other institutions. His articles have appeared in numerous publications. He and his wife, Peggy, traveled as missionary evangelists in Eastern Europe in the 1980s. Today he travels widely speaking on revival, missions, and other themes.

Dr. James O. Davis founded Cutting Edge International and cofounded the Billion Soul Network, a growing coalition of more than 1,000 Christian ministries and denominations synergizing their efforts to build a premier community of pastors worldwide to help plant 5 million new churches for a billion soul harvest. The Billion Soul Network, with more than 400,000 churches, has become the largest pastors' network in the world.

Christian leaders recognize Dr. Davis as one of the leading networkers in the Christian world. More than 40,000 pastors and leaders have attended his biannual pastors' conference and leadership summits across the United States and in all major world regions. During 2007-2011, leaders committed to plant more than 5 million new churches. He has networked with significant leaders from different spheres such as George O. Wood, Jack Hayford, Johnny Hunt, Robert Schuller, D. James Kennedy, Reinhard Bonnke, Chuck Norris, Charles Blake, Barry Black, and others.

Dr. Davis served 12 years leading 1,500 evangelists and training thousands of students for fulltime evangelism as the National Evangelists Representative at the Assemblies of God world headquarters. Ministering more than 45 weeks per year for 25 years to an average yearly audience of 125,000 people, Dr. Davis has now traveled nearly 7 million miles to minister face-to-face to more than 5 million people in more than 100 nations.

Dr. Davis earned a Doctorate in Ministry in Preaching at Trinity Evangelical Divinity School and two master's degrees from the Assemblies of God Theological Seminary. As an author and editor, he has provided:

- *The Pastor's Best Friend: The New Testament Evangelist*
- *Living Like Jesus*
- *The Preacher's Summit*
- *Gutenberg to Google: The Twenty Indispensable Laws of Communication*
- *What to Do When the Lights Go Out*
- *It's a Miraculous Life!*
- *Sign Posts to Armageddon: The Road to Eternity*
- *Beyond All Limits: The Synergistic Church for a Planet in Crisis* (coauthored with Dr. Bill Bright)

His quotes and articles have appeared in *Charisma, Ministry Today, The Challenge Weekly, New York Times Magazine,* and elsewhere.

Dr. Davis resides in the Orlando, Florida, area with his wife, Sheri, and daughters, Olivia and Priscilla. They also have two children, Jennifer and James, who reside in heaven.

James O. Davis may be invited to speak for your church or organization by contacting:

James O. Davis
P. O. Box 411605
Melbourne, Florida 32941-1605
417-861-9999
www.JamesODavis.com

If this book has ministered to you, please prayerfully consider giving monthly support to Cutting Edge International at www.JamesODavis.com. Those who provide monthly support receive a FREE copy of each new book Dr. Davis releases.

To learn more about walking with Jesus Christ or for more information about the author and for additional resources that will strengthen your walk with Jesus Christ, please visit online:

www.JamesODavis.com

How to Become a Christian

Change Your Mind: The first step in becoming a Christian is to repent or change your mind about Christ and sin. To repent is to have a life-altering change of mind concerning your need to live a life of obedience to God. To make a decision to come to faith in Christ that is genuine, one that will stand the test of time, you must have a sincerely remorseful, repentant heart. It is a necessary element. It has been said that *repentance* is the first word of the gospel.

Change Your Heart: If you are ready, all you have to do is bow your head in prayer, repent by sincerely asking Jesus Christ to forgive you of all your sins and to be your Savior as He has paid the price for your sins through His death on the cross, and promise to be as obedient to God's will as you possibly can. It is that simple.

There is no specific way to do it. There is no word-for-word prayer you have to say. All it takes is a repentant heart through faith in Christ with a sincere desire to turn from your former ways and follow Christ.

If you have prayed a prayer of forgiveness and accepted Jesus Christ as your Lord and Savior, you are now ready for eternity in heaven. You are a Christian and will inherit eternal life when you die or Christ returns to this earth to gather His children home.

What do I do now that I've accepted Christ?

- Seek other Christians to fellowship with in a church of your choice that uses the Bible for instruction in holy living.

- Start reading the Bible regularly in order to get to know God better and understand His will for your life.

- Be baptized in water by immersion. If you were baptized as an infant, you need to be baptized again. Baptism is your public acknowledgement of your acceptance of Jesus Christ as your Lord and Savior. Although you can get to heaven without being baptized, Jesus told us we should be baptized just as He was. Follow the Lord's example and do this as soon as possible.

- Tell others about your decision to follow Christ that they may be led to follow in your footsteps. There is no greater accomplishment than to lead another person to Christ!